Tuned In

and

Fired Up

Tuned In and Fired Up

How Teaching Can Inspire Real Learning in the Classroom

Sam M. Intrator

Yale University Press   *New Haven & London*

Excerpt from "Mirror" from *Crossing the Water* by Sylvia Plath. Copyright © 1963 by Ted Hughes. Originally appeared in the *New Yorker*. Reprinted by permission of HarperCollins Publishers, Inc.

Excerpt from "What Work Is" from *What Work Is* by Philip Levine. Copyright © 1992 by Philip Levine. Used by permission of Alfred A. Knopf, a division of Random House, Inc.

"Barbie Doll" from *Circles on the Water* by Marge Piercy. Copyright © 1982 by Marge Piercy. Used by permission of Alfred A. Knopf, a division of Random House, Inc.

Set in Minion Roman type by Keystone Typesetting, Inc.

Printed in the United States of America.

The Library of Congress has cataloged the hardcover edition as follows:

Intrator, Sam. M.
   Tuned in and fired up : how teaching can inspire real learning in the classroom / Sam M. Intrator.
     p. cm.
Includes bibliographical references and index.
ISBN 0-300-10022-1 (cloth : alk. paper)

1. Teaching. 2. Learning. I. Title.
LB1025.3.I584 2003
371.102—dc21

A catalogue record for this book is available from the British Library.

ISBN 0-300-10766-8 (pbk. : alk. paper)

10 9 8 7 6 5 4 3 2

To Jo-Anne, Jake, Kaleigh, and Casey, my inspiring crew

A lowering of vitality clips the wings of youth and exuberance.
—IRWIN EDMAN, *Arts and the Man*

Contents

Foreword

There is no shortage of critics of American public school education. From virtually every corner of our country comes expressions of concern about test scores that are not high enough, behavior that is not orderly enough, students who are not focused enough. We examine our test scores and wring our hands that our nation is losing the education race; Singapore gets higher math scores than we do. The solution to this "problem" is to mechanize and standardize our approach to the improvement of our schools. We seek uniform curricula, a one-size-fits-all approach to school improvement. We specify expectations in terms of standards and woe be the school principal or the teaching staff who fail to meet them. We develop measures of performance as if we could, with the precision of a thermometer, determine just how well our students are doing and we express our joy when this year's test scores are a half of one point higher than they were last year, as if test scores were really substantive proxies for the quality of education our students receive. In a word, we have embraced a reform agenda that was designed for General Motors and have applied it to our schools, all in the name of improved education for our children.

Sam Intrator's book gives us quite another vision, and in this sense, it swims upstream. It could easily be characterized as a tale of romance, a love affair between an astute observer of classrooms and a high school teacher committed to providing educationally vital experiences for his students. Romanticism somehow suffers from a kind of "softness," it conjures up what is mushy, it traffics in the imaginary. Yet, romantic views often touch a spot that is very real for most of us. We profit from portraits of practice that have the capacity to capture the forms of life we ourselves would like to lead. Intrator's volume presents episodes that matter, and not in theoretical abstractions that often conveniently obscure what we cannot describe or explain, but through a language that makes vivid the feel of the place about which he writes.

The lessons, if I can use that word in this context of *Tuned In and Fired Up,* are reminiscent of the best examples of progressive education. First of all, Intrator portrays a classroom that engenders what educationally vital experience looks like, and he has the literary ability to enable us to virtually taste the experience. Second, he helps us understand a soulful side of adolescence, a side that is often neglected by bureaucrats seeking to prescribe educational policies that too often reduce education to narrow attainment targets. Indeed, in policy discourse we often use a language that is as much industrial as anything else. We align our tests with our curriculum, we formulate standards for performance targets, we monitor and measure our outcomes as if they were singular in character. In some schools, young children and teachers are monitored to make sure that they, too, follow the script prescribed. In the process, whatever professional integrity teachers once had is compromised under the press of educational policy.

It is timely, therefore, that American readers be reminded that teaching requires far more than the application of routine techniques to pre-specified ends; teaching, at its best, is a human activity that is more art than technology. Matters of heart matter, and adolescents, in particular, need the space and the support to express those parts of themselves that often get stifled in classrooms where test performance and, at times, indifferent teaching dominate the pedagogical agenda.

This book is significant because it describes in graphic, and I would say, memorable terms what stellar educational practice can be and what such practice yields for those lucky enough to have it. What such practice makes possible is an exhilarating sense of engagement that provides intrinsic satisfactions. It is those satisfactions, rather than the commodified rewards so often used in schools, that provide our best assurance that what students learn in school will be pursued once they leave its portals. We too often forget that what really counts in schooling is not what students can do in school, but what they choose to do outside of school. It is the world in which they live outside of the confines of our academies that serves as the most important field of activity. Getting excited about a point increment in test performance from one year to the next is a symptom of wanting too little from our schools rather than too much. Sam Intrator has given us a compelling portrait of the ways in which educationally vital experiences were secured and he provides a variety of considerations that we might take into account as practitioners and as members of an educational community who in one way or another help shape educational policies.

Excellence in any field is not easily won. In education, it is an especially difficult achievement. Relatively few classrooms, but maybe more than we expect, display the features that Sam Intrator describes in this book. As a result of our own socialization affecting the processes of teaching—socialization which began when we were six years of age—we have a lot to overcome. Sam Intrator has helped us remember—that is, reconnect with—what special moments of educational experience were like, and in the process he encourages us to think about education in ways that penetrate most deeply into that romantic part of ourselves we call our individuality. At a time when standardization is so pervasive in our thinking about how to improve our schools, the message of *Tuned In and Fired Up* is of special importance.

ELLIOT W. EISNER
Stanford University

Gratitudes

One of the privileges of this study was that I had the opportunity to study an artist at work. Almost every day for a year I nestled into my corner alcove and watched Mr. Quinn work to create opportunities for his students to think deeper, see further, and understand more. For his courage and his resolute commitment to this project, I will be forever grateful.

And although Mr. Quinn welcomed me to room 36, his students needn't have opened up to me or embraced this project—but they did. While some were baffled that I would return to high school on my own volition, they were great sports. They were patient with my questions and courageous with their answers. They did their best to help me understand the ebb and flow of their minds and hearts as we traveled through the year. My time with this group affirmed my steadfast belief that despite the criticism society hurls at today's teenagers, I am continually inspired by their compassion, their idealism, and their humor. Students, I have done my best to represent your intelligence, sensitivity, and candor. Thank you.

A side benefit of the project was that as a participant-observer in Mr. Quinn's class, I witnessed many poignant conversations about the great literature that the class read. One day while observing a small group of students talk about Robert Frost's poem "The Road Not Taken," one of the students questioned whether Frost's poem really could apply to their lives because the "walker" in the poem made an important decision without consulting others. She said, "We really don't make important decisions all by ourselves. We live among others." I remember feeling grateful for this insight: she was right. We live our lives and do our work in community with others. This book was not begun or completed in isolation but was accomplished because of the contributions of many. The *road I took* has been lined with good friends and remarkable people to whom I am grateful.

To my mentors at Stanford: Elliot Eisner, your vision for schools and artful practice comprise the constellation of ideas at the center of this book. To the late and wonderful Buddy Peshkin, you modeled for me a life of scholarship lived with integrity. To Edwin Bridges, I've never known anybody who works as fiercely as you do to ask questions that help others become wiser. To Robert Roesser, thank you for conversations that lifted my spirits. To Denise Pope, the seriousness with which you took the voice and ideas of students in your research became the model for my own work.

I am grateful to the team of readers who helped make this book better. I wrote the first version of this book in a writing group with Kay Moffett, Wendy Rosov, and Susan Verducci. They were sensitive when they had to be and always incisive—the core ideas of this book emerged in response to their honest questions. A special thanks to Rob Kunzman, a brilliant teacher and basketball coach whose comments on later versions of the text exemplify why he is so successful with students. To Megan Scribner, a friend who reads with utmost care.

I am also grateful to the team at Yale University Press. Susan Arellano believed in the promise of a book that presents students thinking seriously about their academic experiences. Erin Carter, who came on board at the Press like a captain steering this book to port in the final—but ever-critical—stages: thank you for your insights into the text and your understanding of the difficulties of balancing school, family, and writing commitments. Ali Peterson edited the book with scrupulous attention to both the big ideas and the details. I learned about writing and thinking from her work. Thanks also to Margaret Otzel, who shepherded the book through production.

This is a book about teaching. As such it is informed by my association with a long list of brilliant, creative, and compassionate people: Deb Altman, Robert Bernheim, Lenore Braverman, Adam Bunting, Michael A. Copland, Val Gardner, Joe Greenwald, Marcy Jackson, Rick Jackson, Eddie Katz, Wendy Kohler, Andre LaChance, Noreen Likins, Jim Mangano, Connie Metz, Chris O'Donnell, Parker J. Palmer, Barbara Rossi, Sam Scheer, Suzanne Strauss, and Larry Thomas. I cherish and honor the role you play in my life. I would also like to thank Christine Barbuto and my colleagues at Morgan and Gill Hall. Thank you, as well, to the Smith students who participated in this project: Sky Chandler, Sarah Katz, and Helen Lee.

As the son of two recently retired New York City Board of Education public school teachers, I never had to search far for feedback and wisdom. I'm grateful for the conversations with my dad about teaching and learning. And when it came down to crunch time, whom did I call? Mom. And she read, and read, and reread then did a meticulous job on the index.

To my family, without your support, love, and energy none of this could happen. To my three children—Jake, Kaleigh, and Casey— everyday you give new, wild, and wonderful meaning to the words *tuned in and fired up.* And finally, to Jo-Anne, you are grace and strength personified.

CHAPTER 1

"The Kids Were on Fire"
On the Nature of
Inspired Learning and Potent Teaching

On my thirty-sixth day of being a high school English teacher, I burst out of my classroom at Sheepshead Bay High School in Brooklyn, New York, barely able to contain my elation: "What just happened in there? And how the hell do I figure out how to make that happen again and again and again?" My students had just finished a discussion of how themes woven into Billie Holiday's "Strange Fruit" connected to Jim's mindset in Mark Twain's *Adventures of Huckleberry Finn*. The intensity of their focus, the ferocity of their insights, and the originality of their ideas dazzled me. Those ragtag juniors and seniors were, on this day, rivals in insight and animation to any latte-sipping graduate student as they talked about how the theme of despair permeated *Huck Finn*, "Strange Fruit," and their own lives. The bell rang to end sixth period, and instead of the usual noisy scramble toward the door, nobody moved. We kept at it because the students *wanted* to. Charged with pride and wonder, I remember thinking, "They were on fire! The kids were on fire!"

I went directly to the library and pulled out the black-and-white composition book that had become a travel companion on my teaching journey. I jotted down these notes in response to my experience:

What strange spirit visited us today within this building where most students seem so resistant to really engage in the stuff we're teaching? What pixie sprinkled us with magic dust? Today I witnessed learning and it was more beautiful to me than a thousand Van Goghs. This was why I came to this work. This is what I imagined teaching could be. There have been brief and fleeting moments where we've been focused and engaged, but today some other quality seemed overwhelmingly present: we were awesome. As Devon walked out of the room, ever cool and detached, he stopped, nodded, and gave me a swaggering thumbs up: "Good stuff today," he told me. It's sad how much his sense that something productive and important happened in our class meant to me. I feel like a madcap scientist who pulled twenty nameless potions off the shelf, mixed random dollops together, and it went POOF! How do I figure out how to recreate today's class? I know it's not about formulas, but it's not magic either.

Seventeen years hence I think back on that class as my pedagogic grail. It represents my North Star against which I measure my best hopes and aspirations in my teaching. Any competent teacher who has returned home with clothes dusted by chalk or hands smudged by whiteboard markers knows the force of a moment when the class takes off and students become swept up by a genuine and passionate interest in what they're learning. Perhaps because teaching is such a wild, erratic ride, we give these intensified moments names that emphasize their capricious qualities: the teachable moment, the dream lesson, the masterpiece lesson, or the moment lightning strikes. Longtime English teacher Margaret Metzger wrote about the divine visitation of such moments in her essay "Calling in the Cosmos": "Once my class was reading 'King Lear,' and a thunderstorm crashed down just as we encountered the lines: 'Blow, winds, and crack your cheeks. Rage, blow.' I took the students outside, and we screamed Lear's lines into the storm. I love moments like that!"[1]

As teachers, we live for these moments when our students become beguiled by the subject matter at hand. Other professions have such moments, too. With skill and devotion, on occasion a baseball player can crack a long, arcing home run, a figure skater can nail the triple axel, a poet can compose a verse that feels just right. And on occasion, a teacher can create conditions in a class where students engage in their work with zeal and where the room hums with energy. Maxine Greene describes a goal of teaching as successfully rousing people to poke their heads through what Virginia Woolf calls the "cotton wool of nondescript daily life" and undergo an experience of "wide-awakeness." I like to think of these moments as the times when my students and I plunge through the cobwebs and fog of our everyday routines.

This book systematically approaches these episodes in teaching when the classroom rocks with energy and adolescents find value and meaning in the experience. I am writing about optimal, high-octane moments in the classroom, and I do so as someone who has taught in Brooklyn, Vermont, California, and now Massachusetts. I probe and poke at the anatomy of moments that really work, but still many times I am humbled by the roiling ups and downs of the classroom dynamic. I recognize that these episodes are fragile, infrequent, and elusive—but I also believe that, as educators, they represent our most artistic and enduring triumphs.

One doesn't need to teach for long before realizing that kids are changing all the time. Many students are weighted down by complex issues that deflect our best efforts and render us insignificant in some cases and demanding burdens in others. Likewise, we teach who we are, and sometimes we're tired, listless, and cranky, and other times we scheme up what we think is a smash of a lesson plan only to witness it skid and crash. A former colleague and avid baseball fan used to say, "They prattle on about the difficulty of hitting a baseball and that even major leaguers fail to get a hit seven out of ten times. Well we don't measure classes as hits or misses, but I would venture to guess that teaching teenagers is right up there with hitting against Pedro Martinez or Roger Clemens." Complex, erratic, and frustrating—yes—but sometimes in our classes there are moments of nobility, virtue, and excellence. Larry Cuban wrote: "In teaching, I have experienced the deep satisfactions of connecting to others in ineffable moments, producing odd tingles, even goosebumps, on my back and neck, when a class, small group or individual and I become one—moments listening to students that provided me with insight that upended a conventional idea, moments that forced me to re-think after I had closed my mind's door, moments when my students had touched me deeply. These rare instances are like the resounding crack of a bat that sends a ball soaring into left field or like the graceful pivot to avoid the outstretched arms of an opposing player that allows you to go for an easy layup. These moments I treasure."[2]

This book is about treasured moments of excellence in teaching and learning. It's about identifying and analyzing occasions when teenagers become immersed in their work and undergo a break-through because of a particular encounter with their subject matter. It's about those exalted moments in the classroom when students describe an energy and vitality that is rarely associated with aca-demics. One day, for example, after a freewheeling class discussion on what words and images represent attributes of the American spirit, Victor, all muscles and nervous energy, sat with me and de-scribed his experience in class: "Sometimes, like today, during dis-cussion, I'll be sitting in my chair and I feel like I have leaping insides. I mean I'm listening so hard and trying to think of what I want to say. My energy is intense. I feel like I'm playing football, except I'm sitting in class thinking about the book." Victor's words may lack erudition, but they no less evoke the vigor that is the essence of these moments.

* * *

I've always been fascinated by spans of time that stand out from the inexorable chug of the routine. And I am stirred by artists and thinkers who believe that experiences of virtue and possibility can be achieved even in ordinary lives and within sometimes weary institutions. In my examination of the anatomy of these moments in teaching that stand out from the routine—such as when a student's insides are leaping—I have been guided by three common-sense propositions:

First, most of life whips past us without discrete emotional and cognitive impacts on our consciousness. In the hurly-burly of everyday living we have a limited capacity to extract significance and worth from the vicissitudes of life. In William Wordsworth's "Tintern Abbey" he describes the everyday as a "sad perplexity" of "half-extinguished thought," where "joyless daylight" and the "fever of the world" blunt one's heart and spirit. Ralph Waldo Emerson observed: "To speak truly, few adult persons can see. . . . Most persons do not see. At least they have a very superficial seeing."

These descriptions suggest that much of the subjective reality of everyday experience often unfolds in muted monotone, devoid of genuine passion and awareness. We move through our routines mindless and inattentive to our environment or so overrun by the glut of stimuli that we don't have the capacity to see coherent forms of meaning in ordinary living.

According to these portrayals, men, women, and high school students shuffle through their lives disengaged from the possibilities of intellectual excitement coursing past them. Provocations do not pierce the sometimes insensate condition of teenagers' lives, and they trudge through school oblivious to the mysteries lying within algebra, immune to the beguiling poetry of Emily Dickinson, and weary of the fascinating tale of democracy's genesis. To the student negotiating the pressures and constraints of high school, even the profound and stark meanings in Elie Wiesel's *Night* slip by undetected amid internal and external distractions.

Second, in spite of our inclination to use ethereal language to describe these compelling classroom experiences, their importance is not abstract. I believe they represent triumphs of potent teaching. Such a moment occurs because a teacher cultivated a hospitable space for it to emerge and made critical pedagogical decisions that ushered it into being. We can learn much about the teaching and learning encounter by carefully scrutinizing the anatomy of these inspired moments.

The source of inspiration can be external, something that infuses an idea or purpose into the mind, or it can be internal, such as the result of an awakening. No matter if the rousing prompt is a teacher, the subject matter, or an inner process, inspiration involves the full engagement of the mind.

Annie Dillard, in *Pilgrim at Tinker Creek,* reveals how these moments are not passive, but are active, embodied experiences that must be seized by the individual. She writes: "Catch it if you can. It is early March. I am dazed from a long day of interstate driving homeward; I pull in at a gas station in Nowhere, Virginia, north of Lexington. . . . I am absolutely alone. There are no other customers. The road is vacant, the interstate is out of sight and earshot. I have hazarded into a new corner of the world, an unknown spot, a Brigadoon. Before me extends a low hill trembling in yellow brome, and behind the hill, filling the sky, rises an enormous mountain ridge, forested, alive and awesome with brilliant blown lights. I have never seen anything so tremulous and alive. . . . How can I have not noticed that the sun is setting? My mind has been a blank slab of black asphalt for hours, but that doesn't stop the sun's wild wheel."[3] Dillard's charge reverberates: Catch it if you can. These words pinpoint the essence of inspired learning. It is always there to be caught, secured, achieved—but so often all that's experienced by students is the endless, monotonous blank slab of black asphalt. The reward of catching it is the unconquerable feeling of being tremulous and alive.

An important assumption of this study is that potent teaching can more frequently help students achieve moments of inspired learning. To be potent is to be powerful and influential. Potent teaching, however, is a complex art that involves more than throwing provocative material at students or exhorting them to rouse to life. A potent teacher will skillfully and gracefully create conditions and stage activities that inspire students to have a sustained and meaningful encounter with a subject—because they can.

Third, these moments are not ephemeral flashes, but rather they leave an enduring presence in a learner's life. Our adolescents spend more time in the high school classroom than in any other venue in their lives. The practices and procedures of the classroom are dauntingly familiar to our youth, yet there are moments of fire that occur in this familiar and often tiresome space. I believe these episodes are a paragon of the student-teacher interaction; they are optimal moments when students genuinely enjoy learning and benefit from more than pleasure. In this book I describe events when students tapped into creative strengths, inner resources, and their capacity to work constructively with others. There is educational excellence in these moments, a concept with far greater potential than the sanitized theories of quality teaching that often dominate the educational landscape.

I do not disavow that our schools are beset by problems and sad iniquities, but the enterprise of education remains a hopeful, optimistic venture, and we must keep our spirits vibrant by honoring our triumphs and giving ample public discourse to our successes. We must develop a vocabulary of hope and faith that can serve as an antidote to what feels like relentless critique of the work we do in our schools. Mike Rose tells us that "public education is bountiful, crowded, messy, contradictory, exuberant, tragic, frustrating, and remarkable. We need an expanded vocabulary, adequate to both the daily joy and daily sorrow of our public schools. And we are in desperate need of rich, detailed images of possibility.[4]

*   *   *

I remember one day sitting with a group of teachers and picking up the magazine section of the *New York Times.* There was a picture of a family sitting at a table. Accompanying the picture was a short article that described what the individuals were thinking and feeling in the moment the photograph was taken. I turned to the teachers and asked, "How often would you like to be able to do this during class?" We chuckled because almost every teacher with whom I've ever worked, from the most grizzled veteran to the most idealistic novice, has described the feeling of looking at their students and wondering, "What is in their heads?"

Answering that question is the heart of this work. I wanted to understand not just what students were thinking and feeling when they were in our classrooms, but I wanted to then use what I learned to determine which specific conditions are present when teenagers find inspiration in their academics.

My efforts to answer these questions landed me in Mr. Quinn's junior English class at Stanton High School, a large, comprehensive high school located on the West Coast. The community of Stanton is a well-established bedroom community for a major West Coast city. The school belongs to a sprawling county school system with an open enrollment policy for the high schools, which means that families in Leandro County can enroll their children in any of the seven high schools. The county's population is about 750,000, and slightly more than 50 percent is non-white.

As is the convention with most classroom research, all the names in this book are pseudonyms, and in certain cases, distinguishing characteristics have been altered to protect the anonymity of the students and teachers studied. After observing about 25 classrooms and teachers in an effort to find an appropriate site for this project, I selected Mr. Quinn's junior English class for the following reasons: First, Mr. Quinn was an experienced teacher who ran an innovative and exciting class. Second, his fourth period midlevel junior English class met some important criteria: it was ethnically diverse (60 percent white and 40 percent non-white), had a range of abilities (17 students read below and 15 above grade level), and, most important, the class met right before lunch so I was able to interview students right after class. Third, the project intrigued Mr. Quinn, and he willingly opened up his classroom to me and encouraged his students to speak candidly about their experiences. This was no small risk: the norm of teaching behind closed doors runs deep in high school, and I consider Mr. Quinn's willingness to open his classroom to a researcher an act of exceptional courage.

I began by immersing myself in the daily routines and vicissitudes of Mr. Quinn's classroom. Over the course of one school year, I observed 128 classes and collected a vast archive of classroom data, including more than 120 hours of audiotaped interview data, and I compiled more than 1,400 pages of transcripts. My routine was consistent: Each day, I sat with students during class, recorded my observations in a field notebook, and conducted interviews after class with individual students, focus groups, or Mr. Quinn. I also administered three surveys exploring general classroom and school experiences, exchanged more than 300 emails with Mr. Quinn and students, and collected thousands of pages of student writing, including assignments, journal entries, and homework.

Additionally, many students voluntarily kept "experience journals," where they recorded the peaks and valleys of the school day. During class sessions when Mr. Quinn or I perceived an intensity of focus or emotion, we would distribute index cards in the last minutes of the period. Students would write a short response to a general prompt: "Describe what you were thinking or feeling during class today." These reflective prompts were critical in the data collection.

The soulful Native American writer N. Scott Momaday offered guidance for me as I prepared to document how Mr. Quinn's classroom was experienced. Momaday tells us that to learn about someplace we are to "look at it from as many angles as [we] can, to wonder about it, to dwell upon it . . . at every season and listen to the sounds that are made upon it."[5] I did my best to heed his counsel.

A Glimpse of Life in Room 36

Stanton High School, built about 75 years ago, could never be mistaken for anything but a school, with its stone pillars, wide steps, and institutional lines. Inside the main entrance, a washed-out mural depicting Longhorn cattle and Conestoga wagons dominates the shabby lobby.

Stanton's commitment to being a "traditional school" is apparent in the physical arrangement of many of the classrooms. In almost every one, the desks are aligned in rows facing forward; teachers stand front and center, their voices dominating; students are nearly silent. The walls are painted in antiseptic colors, are devoid of student work, and are barely decorated aside from an occasional promotional poster from a book company; the whole school has an impassive, worn patina to it.

A vivid description of the school and the community was given to me by a student who had written it for an assignment. She thought I might be interested in hearing what students think of Stanton and the "Stanton penitentiary," as one student called it. She wrote: "Stanton High School in Stanton is a long, boring book, a long-lasting obnoxious smell, a rude-awakening gong, a hot flame, a sound wave, a priority, and an alarm clock. Stanton is busy and quiet, cement stairs and uneven ramps, broken windows and tagged up bathrooms and piles of students, stuffy classrooms of large windows letting in gold, backpacks, benches, and tree stumps, and narrow, crowded hallways, and overheads and chalkboards. Its students are stoners, skaters, bookworms, and average teens."

Another student had this to say: "Stanton is one of those places that look all-American on the outside, but when you look inside past the pretty trees, past the proper-looking school, past the kids who look nice, it's really a boring, ugly place."

As you move down the hall from the stark entry, it's like a game of duck, duck, goose. Duck, duck, duck, and so on, but you'll know when you get to the goose—that's room 36. The door is covered with photographs, cartoons, and stickers, and stands out like Dennis Rodman playing basketball in a lawyer's league.

The room itself is a generic space, but probably deeply familiar to most Americans. The speckled, scuffed 12-inch-by-12-inch floor tiles, the efficient glow and perpetual hum of fluorescent lights, the air heavy with an assortment of adolescent odors. I wedge into a seat-desk in the corner of the classroom and notice that the top is furrowed by years of methodical gouging. As I trace the etchings, I remember whittling away my own tedium years ago.

The electronic beep that calls to order the "formal curriculum" has not yet sounded, and the students gather in clutches talking and laughing. The boys have made their way into the classroom, and Arnie, a teenage bodybuilder, lifts up a battered floor fan and airs his underarms. "Thanks for the fucking daisy sniff," calls Arnie's buddy Dave. "Yo, I got gym before this," Arnie explains. Jen drops heavily into her desk and lays a hooded head down across folded arms. Jack, his baggy jeans riding low off his hips, hikes up his shirt to adjust plaid boxers. Verna, who sits next to him, rolls her eyes and says, "Oh gee, Jack, thanks for the view."

With the sound of the bell, Mr. Quinn enters the room. Students promptly slip into desks, reach into bags, throw open books, and generally settle. As he makes his way to a wobbly lectern against his desk, he leans over to talk with Linda. "Hey, where you been?" he asks. She says something I can't hear from the back. He raps her desk with his knuckles, sort of a coach's slap on the back. "Well, I'm glad you're back," he says.

Stepping forward to the lectern, he pulls out the attendance form. He looks up at Arnie and winces. "Thanks," he says while wrinkling his nose. Arnie is still flapping his underarms. The class groans.

Mr. Quinn folds up the sleeves of his blue oxford, and his eyes roam over the class. He is in his mid-thirties and wears a goatee and an earring. As one of the students said, "Mr. Quinn looks like you'd want your English teacher to look like. I mean he's got an earring, and he wears black turtlenecks and looks like the guy holed up in the corner of Starbucks with a laptop computer."

"We've got a lot to do today," says Mr. Quinn.

"Is that opposed to yesterday?" Trey retorts.

An observant comment; Mr. Quinn generally sets class in motion with those words. Students are accustomed to the ritual and recognize that Mr. Quinn uses it to set a boundary and collect their attention. For Mr. Quinn, however, the phrase is more than a hollow transition. He works hard to treat his students as partners in the enterprise, and he's determined that his classroom will be a place where both he and the students will be, in his words, "working hard at learning."

Mr. Quinn himself struggled with high school and often shares his experience of being a resistant and disenchanted student. "I see you looking at me with that grimace and glare," he once said to them after he had just given them an assignment. "I know that look because I used to have it perfected. It meant, 'I'm not buying what you're selling. I'm *not* believing what you're saying. Don't play me.'"

Mr. Quinn uses his own experience in school as a litmus test for much of what he attempts to accomplish with his students. "When I plan, I ask myself, 'Would I, the kid who was slouched in the back of the room, find use and value in this?' When my kids stream into the room, I ask myself, 'Did I reach and make contact in a way that I knew they existed even though they may slide to the back of the room?'"

The class as a whole responds well to Mr. Quinn's invitation to begin. Many students interviewed said that what they like best about Mr. Quinn is his commitment to work hard for and with them. As one student said, "He really tries to learn with us, not just teach us." Another said, "I sometimes get the feeling that Mr. Quinn learns from us. I know he's really smart and wise, but sometimes during class conversation, I just think he's learning from us. Whether he really is, or not, doesn't matter, as much as it seems as if he is trying to learn from us."

Mr. Quinn's energy is legendary among the students. In one student's words, "I would compare Mr. Quinn to a hummingbird. He's always busy, with no time to rest and always active." Another student compares him to a Mexican jumping bean. Aside from his exuberance during class, this nine-year veteran and chair of the department also works with passion and vigor on other professional commitments. With a stack of papers in one hand and a copy of *Huck Finn* in the other, Mr. Quinn begins, "On my way to school today, I found myself thinking about what Huck would say about America and race relations. What do you folks think? I'm really interested in your ideas." And he is—fiercely interested. His students respond.

CHAPTER 2

Spans of Time That Don't Glow
A Portrait of Everyday Life at Stanton High

> Classrooms are powerful places. They can be the sites of numbing boredom and degradation or of growth and connection. In my own educational history, I have known them as both.
>
> —MIKE ROSE, *Possible Lives*

Walking through the hallways, athletic fields, and parking lots of Stanton High, I am often struck by our students' exuberance, yet when these same youth amble into their classrooms, they seem to undergo a debilitating energy drain. I've witnessed this transformation from vitality to lassitude many times: I'll be walking behind a group of students who are engrossed in animated conversation. They are gesticulating and bobbing about, and then they get to the threshold of the classroom and they halt. Before passing through the door, they deflate. All vigor dissipates; struts wilt to shuffles. Likewise is the sequence in reverse. At the end of class, doors fling open and students burst forth, gasping for invigorating air.

It is not news that in many classrooms the mystery and wonder of learning is ground into dust. We all have firsthand experience of wooden teachers and stale classes where time dragged on, leaving our minds passive and disconnected. Indeed, most researchers who have studied how teenagers experience the high school classroom conclude, as did John Goodlad in his massive study of American secondary schools, that the typical classroom possessed a "flat, neutral emotional ambiance [where] . . . boredom is a disease of epidemic proportion."[1]

Although this book focuses on those moments in the classroom when students are exhilarated, it would be naïve and disingenuous to suggest that this constitutes the majority of high school experience. Teenagers at Stanton High School, like at most any high school across the country, were subject to spans of time when learning was just ordinary, when no lightbulbs went on, when time didn't glow. In the interviews, the journals, the focus groups, and in my observations, I heard of classes where students were rarely challenged to think or engage in work that felt meaningful.

*   *   *

Jeff, Jenny, and Bob became my telltales. As a sailor watches the direction and force of the wind, I watched them to discern the ebb and flow of their involvement in class. Over our year together they shared their opinions, perspectives, and insights with me in great depth and with unflinching candor. Their input was not limited to words; I watched this threesome perfect their trademark eye roll and raised eyebrow.

As the year progressed, I came to view their response to school as the quintessential riddle for teachers to decipher: Why do these bright and engaging teenagers find so little in the curriculum that attracts, retains, and excites their interest and passion? Why do they seem to slog through the academic experience of high school exhibiting so little intellectual vitality and motivation?

I conducted one survey in which twenty-seven out of the thirty-two students in Mr. Quinn's class said they were almost always bored in their academic classes. Jenny, a young woman who lugged around a selection of fashion magazines in her backpack to read during class, told me in an interview, "I travel in my mind when I'm in class. There is so much repetition and other stuff that I can't stay there and be sane. I think things. I read things. And then when I can't take it any longer, I say I have to go to the bathroom, and I just walk around. It's not much better in the hallway, but at least I'm moving around. It's like a gerbil in a habit trail."

Bob, a rangy, athletic young man who always looked uncomfortable folded into his chair, described how the teacher's voice mostly floated around as a faraway whisper. He said, "I'm in class and my attention hops around. I'm not concentrating on school. I'm concentrating on cars, girls, or what's going to happen next. Sometimes I sit there and watch Lydia's back, and I'm totally lost in thoughts that I *can* tell you aren't school thoughts. Then sometimes I hear a car rev up outside, and I'm thinking about cars. It's hard keeping track of what's happening in class."

To better understand the pace and character of a typical school day in Stanton, I arranged for several representative students to keep detailed daily logs. I shadowed them through parts of the day and interviewed them at length to document their responses to whatever transpired. Jeff's version of the events best represents what I learned.

Jeff is a seventeen-year-old junior who plays soccer, works as a busboy at a local restaurant, and earns B grades in his classes. He's popular with his peers, well liked by his teachers, and with his typical getup of immaculately creased Gap chinos offset with flamboyant jerseys of various professional sports teams, he always struck me as an apt choice if Norman Rockwell ever magically appeared to paint a scene evoking the essence of twenty-first-century American teenagedom.

Jeff's school day begins at 6:43 A.M. with the sound of the alarm, but he typically hits the snooze button at least once before rising. His morning ritual includes showering and ironing, and then he gulps down a breakfast of Frosted Flakes chased with a cocktail of muscle-building supplements. While he eats he surfs the 105 channels on cable and simultaneously attempts to finish his reading for school.

He lives with his mom and his older sister. Most days, his mom will be off to work by the time he gets to the kitchen, and his sister works nights as a hostess in a restaurant and takes afternoon courses at the community college, so she's never up when Jeff gets ready.

Jeff drives to school. He bought a used Toyota Camry with the money he saved from his summer job at a local restaurant. He still works there two days during the school week and on Saturday nights to "pay for insurance and gas money," Jeff tells me.

"Damn," Jeff mutters as the minivan ahead of him slows and stops at the intersection. Jeff is already late for first period math class. Mr. Jones doesn't usually fuss when he shows up a few minutes late, but Jeff hasn't been on time all week.

He grabs his math text and a spiral notebook and heads into the school. Before opening the door, he gives himself a thorough once over: He pulls his thin gold chain out over his shirt and adjusts the bunching of his baggy pants so they fall over his sneakers just right. He notices a little scuffmark on the toe of sneaker; he wipes it off with his thumb. As a soccer player, a junior, and with a generally amiable disposition, Jeff occupies a niche relatively high up on Stanton's social ladder. As he ambles toward math class, a couple of underclass students walk by and subtly reach for his eyes, but Jeff's hat is pulled so low that he doesn't register their presence. He nods to a few girls whom he knows and gently bumps fists with one of his teammates—this year's official team greeting.

The door to his math class is closed. Everyday at 8:05, when the tardy bell rings, Mr. Jones makes a show of ceremoniously closing the door. He used to lock the door so he could make a scene when students came late, but that created a steady stream of interruptions and mini-encounters, so now he just keeps the door closed as a symbolic, but largely ineffective, deterrent. Jeff pushes the door open and walks into the class. Mr. Jones throws him an exasperated look but doesn't stop talking. Jeff feels a quiver of guilt; Mr. Jones had talked to him about his tardiness, and Jeff had promised to do better. Thankfully, Mr. Jones is still going over the homework that Jeff hasn't done. The routine never wavers in Mr. Jones's class; he starts with the homework, which gives Jeff the chance to do it as the class goes over it. Mr. Jones only occasionally collects the homework, and calls it his "Russian roulette" method of keeping track of assignments.

Jeff hopes that Mr. Jones doesn't put them into groups for the second half of the class. He's got a Spanish vocabulary quiz next period, and he hasn't studied yet. His math book lies open on his desk next to his (now complete) homework, and Jeff quietly pulls out his Spanish word list. He's surreptitious about his multitasking; no need to piss off Mr. Jones.

The last few minutes of class are routinely devoted to getting started on the homework or just socializing, so Jeff asks Jen, who sits next to him, to give him a quiz on the vocabulary words. Once the buzzer rings, Jeff gathers up his stuff and merges into the stream of teenagers flooding the hallway. "Awesome game last night," his friend Jim says to him and gives him the team handshake. The bustle and energy of the corridor feels good. Jeff moves with a swagger and bop to his step, slapping hands, nodding, and grinning. He's moving faster than usual because he wants to get to Spanish class a few minutes before the quiz so he can "set up" his desk before Senora James starts patrolling the room. "Catch you next period," he tells Jim and ducks into class.

"Setting up" involves writing a few choice clues on the desk. Nothing elaborate, just some lightly traced hints sketched on the desk to help trigger his memory. After a few minutes, Senora James comes in saying, "Hola, chicos y chicas." Jeff likes her. "She keeps things moving," he explains. Once the quiz starts, Jeff makes an effort to concentrate. Like most students who travel the middle track of Stanton's tiered academic system—honors, college, and regular— Jeff pays keen attention to his grades. It's important for him to do well enough, and he manages to keep a 3.3 grade point average. The quiz lasts for twenty-five minutes, and once Senora James collects it, she walks over to the VCR and puts in a Spanish soap opera. "I like her because she knows that we're stressed from the quiz, so instead of doing something regular, she puts on something that we can just watch."

Jeff grabs his history text and his English book and heads back down the hall. He's got history with Mr. Cooper, whom Jeff describes as "ultra-boring, but he'll flay you alive for being late," so he rushes off, not even taking time to talk to Laura, who came to his game yesterday. Mr. Cooper likes structure, order, and precision. There's nothing on the walls of his classroom except a few ready-made posters on great moments in American history. He begins every class the same way: "Who would like to recap the reading we had for last night?" Nobody does the reading in the textbook; everybody just gives it a quick scan right then and makes a few comments. As Jeff says, "I like history and arguing about what's going on in the world, but Mr. Cooper chokes all the fun out of it."

Pulling his hat low over his eyes, Jeff slouches down. He begins to feel weary. Last night Jeff worked until 10:00 P.M., came home, played an hour of video games, fired off some emails, and flipped quickly through *Cannery Row* before lying down and thinking about a crazy kaleidoscope of things: his soccer game, what would happen if he asked Laura to the prom, the six homeworks he owes to history class, needing new brakes for the Toyota, the guys at the gym that he knows just started taking steroids, whether he can swing the grades and money for a four-year college. He closes his eyes to a dizzying swirl of concerns. He once described the moments before sleep as resembling the scene in the *Wizard of Oz* where the monkeys come screeching out of the sky.

*   *   *

Like most of the students whom I came to know, Jeff was a young man of deep passion and diverse interests. He was energetic, thoughtful, and playful. When I heard him talk about his dreams, fears, and hopes, he reminded me of how complex the journey of adolescence is in today's world. He was hard at work figuring himself out and learning to understand his place in his peer group, his family, and the world. In his writing, thinking, and conversations, he was trying on ideas and actively constructing a sense of self; yet his openness in school to big ideas seemed to get shucked off like a backpack outside the classroom.

In spite of the fact that teenagers spend the largest portion of their waking hours in classrooms, they rarely enjoy this time or find meaning in their academics. Our teenagers endure classroom life with the same frustration and resignation that teachers might endure a listless and lengthy faculty meeting. For most high school students, classroom activities are largely boring, tedious, and disconnected from their own lives. Just ask Jeff.

CHAPTER 3

Seeing the World in a Plot of Grass
Discovering the Enchanting Power of the Aesthetic

A thing of beauty is a joy for ever:
Its loveliness increases; it will never
Pass into nothingness.
—JOHN KEATS, "Endymion"

One day during lunch I walked into Mr. Quinn's room, and nine students were clustered around the VCR. Arnie had recently started a hip-hop club, and he had drafted Mr. Quinn to be the faculty adviser so it could be a school-sanctioned organization. "We don't need Mr. Quinn to bust out any spins or fresh steps," said Arnie when I asked him why Mr. Quinn. "But we need his room," was the practical reply.

All eyes are focused on the video. "You see that move where he slides his foot back. That's his call-out move," says Arnie. He reaches up and rewinds. "Look. Look. Listen. It's just a little change in the beat, but it's classic."

"I don't hear shit," said Frank. "Whattya talkin' about?"

"Nah, nah, watch again," says Arnie. "It's just a little change in beat. . . . But it's that little bumm, bop, bumm bop. Everytime I see that, I get such a rush. It's like the music and the step together. Here, listen again. You gotta hear the little things!" It's awesome.

Arnie exhorts his fellow dancers to watch and listen more

carefully. He wants them to find a deeper understanding of the music's nuances. Implicit in his advice is the promise of a rich reward for deep and conscious attention.

In this chapter I describe one class when students were assigned a perceptual exercise that led to inspired learning. They were asked to study the aesthetic qualities of a one-foot-by-one-foot plot of grass as if they were poet-scientists, and in the process, students discovered meaning and found intellectual exhilaration.

Awakening to Beauty: A Portrait

The day only dawns to which you are awake.

—HENRY DAVID THOREAU, *Walden*

Today, a respite from the spring torrents has buoyed the collective spirit of the class, and they tumble in from the hallway less sodden and friskier than usual. On days like this, the size of the room seems absurd for thirty-two adolescents and one adult.

Mr. Quinn squeezes by my corner hideaway, throws a grin my way, and pantomimes sweeping sweat off his brow. "Whew, praise to the sun," he intones. Today's lesson addresses John Steinbeck's ability to transform the ordinary detail into a resonant signifier. Mr. Quinn had neither taught *Cannery Row* nor read it before beginning this unit. This meant that he was simultaneously reading the book and designing the activities. In conversation with me he said, "I don't know if I would love this book if I were reading it as a junior in high school, but what I do want to convey to students is how brilliantly Steinbeck celebrates the ordinary in his writing."

An accomplished writer himself, Mr. Quinn marveled at Steinbeck's prose. "It's astonishing what Steinbeck does with the details of Monterey. While I was in the Peace Corps, Lisa [his wife] was in Korea and I was in Algeria. We wrote all the time, trying to share the details and capture the little nuances of our daily life. It's a profound challenge for a writer to evoke the living quality of a place. Steinbeck does that in ways that make your jaw swing open."

Mr. Quinn consistently shared his reverence with the students. On the day he distributed copies of *Cannery Row,* he began by saying, "O.K., wait until you hear this. Everybody open to page one and just sit and listen." He then read: "Cannery Row in Monterey in California is a poem, a stink, a grating noise, a quality of light, a tone, a habit, a nostalgia, a dream. Cannery Row is the gathered and scattered, tin and iron and rust and splintered wood, chipped pavement and weedy lots and junk heaps, sardine canneries of corrugated iron, honky tonks, restaurants and whore house, and little crowded groceries and laboratories and flophouses."[1] He concluded his reading, clearly in awe: "How does a place become a poem, and how does one make a place a poem?"

Silence follows his question, and then with adolescent irreverence, Joseph calls out, "Whoah, deep, Mr. Quinn." The class titters at Mr. Quinn's expense, and he encourages the good cheer by throwing back his head in the manner of a cosmically inclined flower child and playfully saying, "Like, it would be groovy if you could show me the light?"

Once the class settles, Mr. Quinn begins again, "Today we're going to spend some more time thinking about *Cannery Row.* I'd like to follow up on yesterday's lesson, which I thought, as a teacher, was interesting for a lot of reasons. I was ready for a lot more than what happened. I had planned for us to think about how Steinbeck crafts words and description, and while I appreciate those people who commented, to be honest, I felt slightly unsatisfied with both myself and with what we did together. And today, I'd like to come at this idea a little differently."

Mr. Quinn's candor draws students towards him. One day, for

example, he apologized for being slightly unprepared, and I asked a student how that felt. "I've never had a teacher who apologized for anything. That's one of the things that makes me like him. He's real, a real person, unlike some other teachers who are good at criticizing us but who would never say anything like that about themselves."

Mr. Quinn rubs his hands together like a fiendish scientist, which gets a chuckle from the class. He tells them, "But given yesterday's uneasiness, I've got something special planned for today. Instead of languishing in here amid the desks and chairs, we're going out to the baseball field to write." He passes out the assignment and reads: "You must find a place anywhere on the grass in the baseball field or Washington Park and sit there for the period and write about what you see in your immediate domain (e.g., within a two-foot circumference around you). This will be due at the period's end. You should focus on description, on *showing* what you see. The purpose is to think like Steinbeck or Doc, who both want to see the world in all its magnificence, no matter how small. What biologists and writers do is make observations with no judgment. They simply look at the world really closely. They look very, very carefully. Sometimes we think we see, but we don't." Mr. Quinn pauses for emphasis. He then gives the rest of the directions.

> So when I send you out you may say, 'Look, I'm sitting on a two-foot area of grass. It's all green and all the same shape.' 'Big deal,' you may say. But that's not what a biologist would say. They would look at individual blades of grass. They would look at the patterns. They look to see if some were chewed down. Are some of them incomplete? Are some of them just punching through the grass? What are the patterns that emerge from studying the grass? Dig down between the grass and see what types of things can be found there. How do the daisies grow? Are they all the same? What patterns do you have? So take a piece of paper. I'll collect them at the end of the period. We're going to head out to the baseball field, and we're going to find a piece of ground. You

need to sit apart from everybody else, and you really need to find your own space. I want people 10 or 15 feet from each other. We have a whole baseball field; there's plenty of room.

Mr. Quinn sounds like he's giving an inspirational speech. He's excited about the prospects of this lesson. He and the kids have been feeling "locked up and locked down because of the rain." He wants the students to think outside the box, because they're not responding to Steinbeck in the way he hoped.

Mr. Quinn's right. There's been active and almost hostile resistance to the book thus far. From my seat in the back of the room, I've heard a steady stream of complaints about the book, from "This book sucks," to "Can *Cannery Row*."

Mr. Quinn puts on his sunglasses with a flourish, and points his finger toward the door. His intensity resembles that of a football coach leading his players out onto the field before a big game. "Let's go!"

Arnie shoots his hand up, "Yo, Mr. Quinn, yo, Mr. Quinn."

"Yes, Mr. Alum?"

"Do we have to sit on the grass?" Arnie asks, sliding his fingers down the stiletto-sharp crease on his white jeans.

Mr. Quinn grins and says, "You don't have to sit on the grass . . . but you need to stay still and find a place . . . and you need to follow the directions as they're outlined on the sheet."

Once Mr. Quinn heads down the hall, the class dissolves. Julia digs through the recycling bin and comes up with a piece of cardboard to sit on. Travis takes his soccer ball out of his bag. "Writing my ass," he says, and bounces the ball off Emile's head. Joseph pulls out this month's *Car and Driver*, rolls it up, and slips it into the pocket of his oversized jeans. "What's he thinking now?" he says with exasperation. "No way I'm sitting on grass." Susanne rolls her eyes. "What are we gonna do on the baseball field? Write what? I hate this

book anyway." Kobey grins, "Hey, it's better than sitting here all day."
Joseph jokes to the stragglers in the room: "Now boys and girls, just
go out to the field and write about the grass. Be one with the grass."
He clasps his hands together and bows his head in the manner of a
pious monk. I ask Bob what he thinks Mr. Quinn's got planned. "I
think he wants us to look at things carefully. We're going to try and
be writer-scientists. I don't know. This is kinda strange."

Out on the field, Mr. Quinn says, "Try and give yourself some
room. This is an individual exercise. Randy, if you can, tear yourself
away from Lilia. Travis, stay in the outfield."

Reluctantly the students distribute themselves across the mani-
cured field. As Mr. Quinn surveys the field I can see him becoming
impatient with their antsiness. His voice bristles. "Craig—Do not, do
not, sit next to somebody."

Craig looks over and says, "Sorry, Mr. Quinn."

"What are we supposed to do?" asks Linda. Her head's thrown
back, and her shirt is rolled up past her midriff. "Write what?"
she asks.

"OK, folks, come on," says Mr. Quinn. "I've asked you to stake
out a one-by-one piece of field and treat it the same way that Steinbeck treated Monterey. Write about whatever you see in your immediate environment. Just write."

Vincent sits down heavily and leans back against one of the
stately trees that line the field. "Hey, anybody know if this is a spruce
tree?" Arnie calls over to Mr. Quinn: "Is it O.K. if I write about
something other than the grass?" Dave answers, "Shhh, shut your
fucking mouth." Arnie laughs, and Dave says, "I'm gonna kick your
ass if you ask one more question and interrupt the forty minutes of
sleep I'm planning on getting." He jams the brim of his hat down
over his nose and lies still except for a blade of grass bobbing about
in his mouth.

Arnie solves the grass-stain dilemma by returning to the class and lugging a chair out. "I don't do grass," he says regally. Other students look like they're getting comfortable and enjoying the sun.

"Would you guys stop already! C'mon, I can't write with all this noise," says Lilia. "Yeah, cut the shit," says Randy emphatically. "You're messing with my creative flavor." Soon the class is working, Mr. Quinn sits down on the edge of the outfield and begins his own writing. I, too, sit down and turn to my notebook:

> The sun seems to have cooked the cranky edge off the group. They look relaxed splayed out across the field, but they're writing with intensity. Lilia's sitting on her knees with her nose buried in the grass. Joseph studies the spruce tree, his hand caressing the bark. Susanne's lying on her back, eyes closed, soaking in the sun, and then she jumps up and begins scrawling away in her book. She walked out to the field as if it were an outdoor latrine; now she looks beset by the muse. Mary's shoes are off, and her toes are wiggling around the grass. A raspy fence rattles, and the field caretaker pushes a wheelbarrow and chalk liner out onto the field. He looks around quizzically, perhaps searching for an adult. He begins to push the wheelbarrow toward first base, but stops and shakes his head. He leaves the wheelbarrow standing between home and first and heads back off the field.

The class writes for twenty-five minutes, which was the longest uninterrupted parcel of writing I witnessed all year. As I look out across the diamond, I'm reminded of a phrase I once heard used to describe Graig Nettles, the sensational, panther-like third baseman of the New York Yankees during the 1970s. A radio announcer said, "He waits for the ball simultaneously relaxed and alert." I've rarely seen this combination of serenity and attentiveness at work in schools.

Slowing Down the Whirl of School

With our eye made quiet by the power of harmony . . .
We see into the true life of things.

—WILLIAM WORDSWORTH, "Tintern Abbey"

Currere, the Latin root of *curriculum*, refers to a course or a racetrack, and in our schools we intend to run it fast. Our language about learning and teaching reveals our predisposition to the hare rather than the tortoise: we seek the fast track, we learn to cram, we have accelerated schools where we emphasize coverage and pursue efficiency.

Speed is a virtue in education; yet an outcome such as that in the baseball field comes only when the students slow down. By slow, I do not mean what we normally connote as slow in educational circles: stunted, perseverating, remediating, lethargic, or elementary. But when we put the brakes on the world as it rushes by, we can have a "slow experience," by which I mean attending to our environment with awareness and care. Slow experience is concerned with process rather than productivity. Its end is engrossment. An anecdote illustrates its basic precept:

When I was in a college poetry class, we had just started reading Percy Bysshe Shelley's complex poem "Mont Blanc." A student who was frustrated by the impenetrable syntax and elusive symbolism of the poem shot his hand upward. He was clearly miffed. "Yes," said my professor.

"How do *you* read this poem?" the student asked in a voice tinged with pique. "It will take forever, if we sit and think about every line."

"How do I read it?" my professor responded. "Slowly. So slowly that I linger on each syllable. In order to crack it open and know its beauty and wisdom I must, and you must, dance slowly with Shelley and his words."

Now that the students have settled in, a palpable change is evident in the outfield. Things are quieter, more serene. They have surrendered to the experience. Vincent, earrings gleaming in the sun, reclines against the tree. He stands up and traces his fingers down its coarse bark. He's a four-sport star who once told me that he thinks he has an attention disorder. He later told me that on this day he became "lost in the texture of the bark." Linda, her white elevator pumps off, is rubbing her bare feet against the grass. She stops, writes, glides her toes over the grass, and writes again. Later she told me that she was "reading the grass with her feet," which was something that she had done when she was younger. Trey, who had originally mocked the assignment, twirls a blade of grass, scrutinizes it from every angle, and laces it into a ring. He later said he was trying to envision what the grass looked like from the perspective of the ant that had clambered over his sneaker.

In the interviews I conducted immediately after class, students described feeling "intense and focused" and "being into it." It seems that as they concentrated on their plot, the distractions faded away, and the kids became still, quiet, almost solemn. The hustle and bustle of their typical mode retreated, and in its place was what I would describe as contemplative presence. This wasn't placid torpor, but intense concentration. With about seven minutes remaining in the period, Mr. Quinn walks over to me and whispers, "They really took to this. Look at them go. They are completely absorbed," he says. "I wonder if they realize class is almost over," says Mr. Quinn, glancing with satisfaction at his watch.

Jerry, a young man who responded to my question of what he was good at by saying, "I kick ass in Nintendo," provided a thoughtful description of what the students experienced. "At first I sat down and was like, what the heck, English class? Then I was watching the other students, and they were getting into it. Susanne was a trip, she was rubbing her hands through the grass and then writing, and that sort of convinced me to take it a little seriously. So I started to just look and look at this little plot of ground. All of a sudden it jumped out at me that this grass was a world, a universe. There were bugs, flowers, and specks of pollen. There was this rockin' world in front of my nose, and I was like, 'Wow, some other entity could be looking down at Stanton High, and I would be as significant as the beetle I watched crawl across my space."

Jerry's response points to some key features of this experience. First, he, and many other students, followed a similar script that began by deriding Mr. Quinn's plan as unconventional and voicing resistance to its intent. As they often were when Mr. Quinn tried something atypical, they were skeptical and hesitant. Their reluctance to be freewheeling and open-minded always struck me as odd; they were emphatic about wanting hands-on activities and adamant that the typical classroom modes were hopelessly tedious and boring. What seemed to happen in Mr. Quinn's class was that a high-status kid would acquiesce and begin to participate, and the rest of the class would follow suit. Indeed, Jerry notes that seeing Susanne participate convinced him to at least give it a try.

Second, once Jerry decides to participate, he focuses his attention. He begins to use his mind and his senses in ways that yield rich, textured data about the world. He moves from a blunt, imperceptive encounter with the plot of grass to one where his full sensory apparatus is tuned in and active. It is an experience of heightened perception. A technical definition of perception describes it as a sophisticated interplay of physical and psychological factors that occurs when our sensory apparatus picks up information from our visual, gustatory, olfactory, tactile, and auditory systems and makes meaning of it. The information netted from our sensory organs is what we rely on to construct our world. As Elliot Eisner, a professor of education and art, tells us, "We literally get in touch with the world through our increasingly refined ability to experience the qualities of the world we inhabit."[2]

When Jerry and the students look at, touch, and listen to the plot of grass, they move from cataloguing the elements—grass, ants, dirt—to seeing the tract as a universe teeming with aesthetic qualities. In *Art as Experience,* John Dewey's description of the difference between an act of recognition and an event of perception helps explain what students experienced in the exercise. For Dewey, "Recognition is perception before it has a chance to develop freely. In recognition there is a beginning of an act of perception."[3] Recognition is "bare identification," labeling what one encounters in the world in a way that "involves no stir of the organism, no inner commotion."[4] If recognition is passive, then perception is the active creation of meaning. As philosopher Regina Leffers tells us, "When we perceive, we do not merely recognize, but see with fecundity."[5] This kind of seeing produces imaginative insight. It is active and evocative, not passive and inert.

I give here several examples of student writing that detail events of perception: "A ladybug crawls through the forest of blades getting stuck. The sun shines on its tomato-colored back as it squirms to become unraveled from the trap of grass it is in. Two wings come out and it flies away. . . . The power of the ladybug to fly away is a great power." Another piece probes at issues of evil and innocence. "Sitting here in the park brings back memories of days long ago. Chasing after the ice cream man, walking to the public pool, and watching lovers lay on the blanket of grass. But I have pity on the playground: an innocent place by day and a witness of evil by night. The blades of grass that comfort children's bare feet also soak up the blood of fights. The slides once kissed by the sun now are painted over by thugs proving a point to nobody who cares. Innocence will always be threatened by time."

When I read the students' writing after that class, I was struck by the dramatic tone in many of the essays; these were adolescents thinking about life, death, freedom, even finitude. Their descriptions reminded me of the romantic construct of epiphany, which is an instant of consciousness when an ordinary object comes into sharp focus, yielding robust insight. The philosopher Charles Taylor describes the epiphany as "a manifestation which bring us into the presence of something which is otherwise inaccessible, and which is of the highest moral or spiritual significance."[6] The literary critic Morris Beja defines the epiphany as a "sudden spiritual manifestation, whether from some object, scene, event or memorable phase of the mind—the manifestation of being out of proportion to the significance or strictly logical relevance of whatever produces it."[7]

Trey's description of his experience highlights several of these ideas. As we walked back to the school building, I asked him what he thought about the class. He told me that he couldn't remember ever doing anything quite like this. He also said, "Mr. Quinn told us we were going to think like John Steinbeck. What we usually have to do is learn what Steinbeck or some historian said. We don't learn to be like them." He continued: "The experience was kind of weird. Sort of like staring at one of the fuzzy designs at the mall that you have to keep on looking at before it suddenly clears up. At first, I looked at the grass and saw grass. Big shit. I looked again and saw grass, and then I started to see different things, hear different things, and then smell things that I never noticed before. I noticed, like, the grass blade gets thicker toward the bottom, and then I started to see these weeds, which stood out like loners in the school. Sometimes I feel like that here at Stanton, which is why I'm transferring next year."

Trey's remarks are a trenchant critique of how our schools do not value the development of perceptual skills. He points out that we attend more to learning and processing what others say instead of developing the capacity to attend to what we observe and experience. To emphasize this point, I quote a student's note to Mr. Quinn at the end of the year: "My favorite experience of the year was when we went to the baseball field to set our minds free and write anything: from the ant on the ground, to the cloud in the sky. This was the first time (at school) I was able to sit and see and write anything."

Trey's description also reveals the process by which he expanded his ability to pick up sensory information. His initial encounter operated in the habitual realm, where the characteristics of the grass plot were unseen. As he observed with more focused attention, he began to differentiate between the mass of grass and the individual blades. Further, he noticed the taper and shape of a specific blade. This discernment of the refined attributes of an object suggests that Trey has entered the realm of sharper sensitivity. He used his olfactory and auditory senses to "read" the plot of ground. And from another account, "The sight of the field is not the only thing that comes to mind. The distinct smell of the newly cut grass and the cool breeze that has been freshened during its travels through the surrounding fernwood trees. . . . The sounds of birds longing for their providing mother fill your ears. . . . Their sweet noises are polluted by the distant roar."

In the last part of Trey's commentary he compares the weeds in the field to the loners at school, an example of how attending quietly and carefully to an object can lead to insight into one's own life. Encounters with the aesthetic properties of an object can influence our understanding of and experience in the world. When our encounter is marked by more than mere recognition, we can experience insight that informs and shapes our internal life. Trey's musings on his place at Stanton shows how one's life can transact with an object during an aesthetic encounter.

A poem written by Jen follows a similar trajectory:

> I saw nothing
> I see what everyone else sees
> Green, Green, Green Grass
> Some long, some short
> some with leaves, some without
> But wait
> I see beneath.
> I see much more now
> More of life
> I saw nothing then.

Jen's poem is about epiphany. It begins starkly: "I saw nothing." The line can be read on two levels. First, it expresses the resistance to the assignment felt by many students at first, and it bluntly states that despite the explicit instructions, she saw nothing. A second interpretation reveals a kinship with Dewey, specifically, his observation of how we employ our senses to understand the world. In *Art as Experience* he writes: "We see without feeling; we hear but only a second-hand report, second hand because not re-enforced by vision. We touch, but the contact remains tangential because it does not fuse with qualities of senses that go below the surface."[8]

The first line categorizes the grass; it considers only the most superficial qualities of the object. Jen's repetition of "Green," however, suggests that she held her gaze long enough to discover something else beyond seeing the grass as grass. Her perception is heightened; she differentiates between size, color, shape, and texture. The outfield is no longer a swatch of homogeneous green. There is a pause in the phrasing before she shares her insight. "I see beneath / I see much more now" is testimony to her expanded frame of reference. The phrase "More of life" suggests that the insight gained probed at the existential realm. Her final line, "I saw nothing then," repeats the sentiment in the first line and conveys an awareness of perceptual growth.

Becoming a Poet-Scientist:
A Case Study

Most students in room 36 have a single, fairly stable group of friends, but Lilia crosses boundaries among cliques with grace. "I try not to be totally predictable," she said, and her commitment to variety takes many forms. She's one of the few young women in the class who takes on multiple personas in school. Occasionally she seems the fragile, overwhelmed adolescent girl. Other days, she has the brazen confidence of a zealous intellectual. Sometimes she comes to school in weathered jeans, an oversized sweatshirt, and a baseball cap turned awry. Other times she'll strut in with a miniskirt and heels.

On the day of the lesson in the outfield, Lilia came to school behind in the reading. "We were supposed to be up to chapter three, and I tried—but god, the book sucked. I mean who cares? I did try to read, but it was just so boring that I couldn't go on any farther." Lilia's a conscientious student who prides herself on being organized and up-to-date with Mr. Quinn's assignments. "I may fall behind sometimes in my other classes, but I always try and stay on top of things in English, so I was glad that we were going outside—even though I thought it was pretty weird at first." Lilia describes her experience during the lesson:

> We went out to the baseball field and everyone was sitting on the grass. I chose to sit on the dirt, or on the border of the dirt and the grass. . . . And so I was sitting there, and I thought about it for awhile, and I was going to write a paper about what I saw, because that's what Mr. Quinn said he wanted. But as I sat there and thought and looked, I sort of felt like I needed to write something other than an essay. I never had written any poetry before, but I felt like I needed to say what I wanted to say in a different way. I was trying to decide if I wanted to write about, like, the trees and the air, and then I looked down, and there was just the dirt and

the grass. I could describe each little pebble; they were just like the little pebbles that made this whole baseball field, and how each one was different, each one had a different characteristic to it. There was a little ant walking by at one point, and it was just how his world was so small, and yet he was in such a great, huge area compared to his size. And when you're by yourself you can think more about what's going on; your thoughts are more of yours rather than when you're sitting in the classroom and you see the posters and stuff on the wall, but they're not really yours. And so I thought how it affected me, how just sitting there—I had never thought about a baseball field, the dirt on a baseball field before, or anything like that. I played second base for nine years of my life, and I had never actually looked at the dirt. This was ground so familiar, I had walked over every grain of dirt, but today I saw it again totally differently.

Lilia wanted to render her experience through poetry, but she felt compelled to ask Mr. Quinn's permission: "Mr. Quinn, is it O.K. if I write this as a poem? I know that you said, essay, but . . ."

Mr. Quinn answers kindly. "Lilia, that would be terrific. I just want you to focus on bringing to life the details of your plot. Whatever mode works best would be great."

"Thanks, Mr. Quinn," she says returning to her paper.

Arnie, sitting in the chair ten feet away, says softly, "You go, poet woman."

"Shut up, Arnie."

Lilia's poem, which Mr. Quinn said "captures all that he had hoped to evoke in this lesson," follows:

> Each pebble, each stone
> With a different story to tell
> Some mud red, others as pale as bone
> Large ones, small ones, even too small to see
> Are mounded together in this field
> Broken twigs, dried out needles from nearby trees
> Litter the soil
> Unconscious blades of grass try to sprout

Each blade trying to survive
While most are brown and drying out
The sunlight hits so bright
The entire ground glows
Showing the significance of each object
Underneath the soil gets darker and moist
Like cutting into an unripe orange
Dig deeper and still you find stones
Some even shine and sparkle
Fooling someone to believe they're gold
Precious enough each one is different

A footstep?
Ruins the wholeness of the soil
It's nature
The birds chirping
The bugs clicking
A lonely ant strolls by
In reality you would see it
As where second base belongs
On a baseball field.

Lilia begins the poem with a couplet about the significance of mindful attention to the particular: "Each pebble, each stone / With a different story to tell." She recognizes that distinct elements can have separate narratives. Lilia engages with the objects before her in the spirit of Steinbeck's aphorism in *Cannery Row:* "The thing becomes the word."

The next section details the process of differentiation. She considers the pebbles' size, color, which she calls "pale as dry bone," and configuration. The poem inventories the plot's features, including the surface, the effects of external forces, and the sensations encountered underneath the ground. Lilia's poem conveys her keen state of wakefulness. All of her senses are alert; she sees, hears, and feels more, and through metaphor, she even tastes and smells.

The poem begins with Lilia's recognition of the narrative potential of an ordinary object, and it concludes with the recognition that her observations are affected by what Dewey calls her own "background of past experiences." When she talks about the last line of her poem during an interview, the intermingling of biography and the external world is apparent. "In the last line: 'As where second base belongs / On a baseball field,' I was trying to say that even though I fielded thousands of balls on that same ground, I never knew it. Second base belongs there, but so does all the many things I observed in the poem. It was like two different ways to be at second base. I always knew it as second base, but now I know more carefully."

The assignment affected Lilia deeply. "I learned something really important that day. I mean I learned I could write poetry and say things poetically, but I also learned how to look at things differently," she said in an interview four months after the lesson. Lilia strives to replicate the experience. One particular conversation with Lilia is revealing. I asked her if she had written any other poems since that day at the field. She answered:

One day I was sitting at work and it was raining. It was a depressing Saturday morning, and I was feeling rotten. I work in a floral shop, and on a rainy Saturday morning there's really not a lot to do. I was tapping my fingers on the front counter, and then I began to think of how fun it would be to just sit there and write a descriptive poem just because I learned how to do it, so why not? I thought of *Cannery Row* and the poem I wrote about second base, and I just started to sit there and feel. I sat there and heard the rain. I smelled the scent of a rainy day and the scent of the store. I could see the gray skies and hear the water running off the roof, the hum of the freezers, and the buzz of the gnat in my ear. Even though I've worked there for a long time I think I really began to smell the many different scents of the store and how all the flower smells mix. And I then just described my whole setting around me. And I included things like there was a kid on the street outside walking by and arguing with his parents, and I wrote it.

I then asked: "What's the effect of being able to see all that detail?" She answered: "It makes you think more about it. You realize a lot more than just being there. You appreciate being there more. It's like you're not just walking by your life; you'll remember it better, like I can remember that day, like that day at work, I remember it perfectly, and I realize a lot more things about the store and other parts of my life. I realize the different things there, the different cracks in the building, the smells, the sounds of the people walking past. You just realize things that are there that you never have before, and it kind of affects you a lot more."

What can we learn from this case study? First, Lilia's experience during that class lit her up. She was inspired to use faculties that rarely get called on in school. In the process of mindful examination, she enjoys developing a "poet's eye," as she calls it. Second, she found writing the poem to be exhilarating. Third, the experience made an impact on Lilia. She speaks passionately of how this class opened up new ways of both seeing and responding to the world. In her end-of-the-year portfolio she writes: "This year's English class not only helped me grow in becoming a better student, it also made me grow as an individual. When I look at certain objects, read small articles, or even just sit down and think, my thoughts go deeper than they ever have in the past. . . . This portfolio shows how much I have gotten 'better,' and if I look deep enough I can see."

Cultivating the Aesthetic in the Classroom

Why was this lesson such a success? Why did the students become so swept up in the experience? In my analysis, three components of the event stand out as significant. First, I examine the classroom milieu nurtured by Mr. Quinn. Second, I consider the choice of subject, that is, the plot of grass, and specifically, I explore the use of nature as a text. Third, I discuss how solitude and space provide students room to exercise their creativity.

The Perspicacious Ideology in Room 36

In a six-year study of premier corporations, two organizational theorists, Jim Collins and Jerry Porras, discovered that every one possessed a "fervidly held ideology" that pervaded the company's practices.[9] "Like the fundamental ideals of a great nation, church, school, or any other enduring institution, core ideology in a visionary company is a set of basic precepts that plant a fixed stake in the ground: 'This is who we are; this is what we stand for; this is what we're all about.' Like the guiding principles embodied in the American Declaration of Independence ("We hold these truths to be self-evident") and echoed eighty-seven years later in the Gettysburg Address ("a . . . nation, conceived in Liberty, and dedicated to the proposition that all men are created equal"), core ideology is so fundamental to the institution that it changes seldom, if ever."[10]

As in one of these big-time companies, in Mr. Quinn's classroom, too, several core ideologies were evident. The success of the lesson in the outfield can be attributed to one fundamental ideology that I recognize as the perspicacious spirit. It is one of Mr. Quinn's core values, and it permeates the culture of his class.

Explicit expressions of the perspicacious spirit can be heard in his directions to students. "Read very carefully. Pay attention to the way the words interact with each other." Sometimes while they're watching a film or listening to a recording, Mr. Quinn will stop and rewind a passage and say: "Here, let's look again, and this time really focus in on what's happening. Let's uncover what's going on." He encourages the class to delve deep, and he discourages myopic seeing. One day a student mentioned a passage from *Huck Finn*. Mr. Quinn responded: "Great, thanks for bringing this up. This is a great, pow-

erful, all-important line in literature, and what happens is most
people barely blink. If you don't savor lines like this and probe them,
then why read at all?"

Even before the first class ever met, Mr. Quinn conveyed the
message that he found sustenance and power in small details. His
summer letter to students began: "It is August as I write this and the
summer thunderstorms here in Amherst, Massachusetts, have begun to leave in their wake these calm hours in which I think of our
year ahead." As an opening communiqué, it's rich with meaning.
Mr. Quinn introduces himself as contemplative and attuned to nature. Throughout the year, Mr. Quinn reinforced this core ideology
by sharing anecdotes relevant to thinking and learning. "Before we
start, I just wanted to share something that I noticed while driving to
work." Other times he would share his own thought process with the
class. One day he read aloud to the students Philip Levine's poem
"What Work Is." He began: "We stand in the rain in a long line
waiting at Ford Highland Park." He stops and seems lost in thought.
"Every time I read this, it makes me think of my father. If I think
about it deeply enough it transports me, so to speak."

Mr. Quinn is generous with praise for students who pay attention to details. Collins and Porras point out that in successful companies, the recognition system tightly fits the core ideology. This is
true in room thirty-six as well. The day before the lesson in the
outfield, Jerry makes this observation about Steinbeck's chief theme
in *Cannery Row*: "Steinbeck sucks up all the perceived bad stuff. The
stuff that is on the surface bad, like the fact they are prostitutes and
bums, and then the Word makes them more than just 'bad'; it gives
these people more, or makes them more, than just bad stereotypes."

Mr. Quinn responds with a whistle: "Whew, that's really deep
and perceptive, Jerry. I like how you mined meaning from the words
in the text. That's a really great observation. I hadn't seen that before." Responses like this reinforce his core practice.

Mr. Quinn believes deeply that all his students have the capacity to respond to art, literature, and experience in ways that provoke preconceived notions, inspire fresh insights, and invite more acute understanding of their world. Although many students initially responded to the assignment in the field with skepticism, they all ended up giving a good faith effort. Their willingness to do so can be attributed to both their respect for Mr. Quinn and their honor of the core ideology. "While it seemed kind of goofy at first, I tried it. I know looking closely is something that we've talked about a lot in here, so I sort of played along at first and then sort of got into it."

Nature as Text for the Aesthetic Experience

To be in touch with nature in the open air is of the greatest importance to the young.

—FRIEDRICH FROEBEL

The study of the natural world has long been regarded as a valued educational resource, but does a plot of grass constitute nature? In *The Prelude*, Wordsworth celebrates nature's capacity to create a "heart joyous" that stirs "trances of thought" and deep insight. Many students suggested that just being outside in the fresh air stirred their muse. They were eager to write and think. One student pointed out that "hearing the birds, smelling the grass, and feeling the soft, damp ground got me in the mood to write." A few others said that they enjoyed the assignment because "sitting on the grass with a journal gets one in the mood to write more than sitting in a room with thirty students and a hard plastic seat." Another offered, "There's so much to write about when you're sitting there looking at the ground. I usually sit in class and have nothing to write about in the journals. Once I sat down I just felt like I wanted to write."

The assignment also showed the students how to think about

nature as a text. This novelty intrigued them but it also offered them an opportunity to scrutinize the ordinary—in this case, the grass. They've all walked past, over, and through the field, but they never paid attention to it as a text to be read or a setting to be studied. Jason said it best: "This is where I play baseball. I didn't see it as anything else." The task demanded sharp attention, and when the students do focus, the field opens up to reveal a text teeming with features. Nattie tells us: "I sit on the grass. The ordinary grass that I walk over every day without noticing. Right in front of me is grass. Green grass that I might have stepped on before. There are many shades to this grass. Only the tallest blades move with the slightest wind blown. . . . There are these tiny plants that almost look like an unfilled Christmas tree. . . . Clear raindrops sit on the tips of the grass." What's important to note in Nattie's description is how the grass expands into a differentiated and textured entity. Her full attention to the object yields a fresh awareness of something familiar. It is a resonant moment for Nattie—one that both delights and educates her.

The assignment gave students free rein to unleash their feelings, but most of the class wrote about issues of the heart and spirit only near the end of their essays. A fascinating pattern emerges. Students began their pieces with descriptions of empirical phenomena: beetles, grass, clover, dirt. But these stark observations appear to have triggered more complex ideas, such as how the "sun feeds the grass," "how ants live in a community and lug food to their home," "how stalks of new grass emerge from clumps of dead grass," and "how nature can bounce back against the footprints of man." Many students elaborated on these themes, and by the essay's end, they had extended their focus to the wider world. They wrote about how, in the grass, the drama of life, death, freedom, and community are played out. More than half of the essays compared the world within the blades of grass to life at Stanton High.

Designing Time for Solitude in the Hurly-Burly Curriculum

Solitude is the place for contacting the deeper springs of self.

—PHILIP KOCH

When I looked across the outfield midway through the writing assignment, I was struck by the distance between students and the privacy the environment afforded them. Schools are crowded, hectic places. Educational researcher David Hargreaves likens students to "frantic passengers" at an overcrowded airport.[11] Schools are not serene, and there's little privacy or personal space. Some schools even have no stall doors in the bathrooms.

In Mr. Quinn's classroom, thirty-two students and the teacher occupy approximately four hundred square feet. During a writing assignment, your desk and what you write is visible to at least three others. The day before Mr. Quinn brought students to the outfield, he arranged the class in a circle to explore the question, "In what way are you more than a teenager?" Elbows brushed elbows during the assignment, and there was no private space to ponder this penetrating, personal question. One student said, "I hate this. I feel so cramped." Some students casually crooked their arm around the paper, and others flipped their papers over as soon as Mr. Quinn reconvened the class for discussion. A hand went up, "I loved the question, but Jeff was sitting next to me, and there was no way I was going to write about what was really on my mind."

Conversely, in the field, students enjoyed "stretching out." One young woman told me that she writes only on her bed where it's "private and where I can lay down and think." And from another, "I thought it was nice and refreshing to go outside for once and get out of a stuffy classroom. I get deeper into my writing, and since no one was next to me and could be looking over my shoulder, I could write whatever I wanted."

These comments attest to the conditions that many people find necessary for contemplation. In his book *Solitude: A Return to Self,* Anthony Storr explains that "the capacity to be alone thus becomes linked with self-discovery and self-realization; with becoming aware of one's deepest needs, feelings, and impulses."[12] Although the excursion to the outfield was not a solitary retreat, it did foster better conditions for contemplation: space and relative solitude. As Trey said after I asked him why he liked the lesson so much, "Lounging out and thinking. Heck, I do that all the time in my bedroom or my car."

Mr. Quinn began the class that day hoping that students would learn to see the world like Steinbeck does, like a poet-scientist. At the end of *Cannery Row,* Doc is by himself in his kitchen, tuned into the sounds of the sea, the feel of the water, the smell of the froth whipping off the waves, and he speaks aloud to himself, "Even now, I know that I have savored the hot taste of life." On this day, like Doc, the gang in room 36 savored a taste of life, and learning.

CHAPTER 4

Forging Community
An Episode of Deep Connection

> Real education depends on the contact of human living souls with human living souls.
> —JOHN STUART MILL, letter to Rev. Stephen Hawtry

"It's kind of sad that we always talk about 'keeping it real' and 'being true to each other,' but then we barely know anything about each other. We're in class with these people, but it's all on the surface, and it's almost always just about posing," said Mia during an interview when I had asked her to tell me about her classmates. She began by naming students that sat next to her: "Jeff—he plays soccer. Jen is a cheerleader and drives a blue Escort. Kim is in theatre, and I went to elementary school with her." She stops, shakes her head, and looks at me, "I guess it's pretty weak that I barely know them, but then I know that nobody really knows me either."

In educational circles we understand the need to build a sense of community in our schools, because genuine learning and effective teaching are more likely to occur when we belong to a community that cherishes nurturing, listening to, and caring for each other. The promise of community is a nurturing space where we can stretch our minds with fellow learners and do so in ways that reveal our true selves.

In this chapter I explore one class when students felt particularly connected with one another. The philosopher and educator John Dewey calls this experience of connectedness the greatest human good. A few days after this particular class occurred, I asked Mia if anything had changed about the way she felt about her classmates. She said, "I can't help but smile at them now when I see them. It's like we shared something special together. It was bigger than just a class, because now in some way we belong to these people."

A Portrait of Coming Together in the Classroom

"Arnie, Arnie, Arnie," chanted the class. Several friends of Arnie's—the so-called Testosterone Crew—were stomping their feet, and Frank, the student who always needs to be more dramatic than the rest, performs a loud drum roll on the desk. Arnie springs up and lifts his arms above his head like a weightlifter flexing for the judge, pirouettes once, and says, "All right, I'm ready." Owen calls out, "Yo, Arnie, what are you gonna do, breakdance for us?" In response, Arnie gives a slick move. "Woof, woof, woof," barks the class, these days the preferred expression of adolescent approval.

Mr. Quinn, with an amused half-smirk, says, "O.K., we've got what should be a special day ahead." Arthur calls out, "No pressure, no pressure." Emily, sitting in the front row, waves her hand vigorously. "Yes, Emily," replies Arnie with exaggerated geniality. He's hamming up his teacher persona and perhaps having a little fun at Mr. Quinn's expense. "Sir, Sir! Please, sub teacher, can you write your name on the board?" Arnie nods and grabs a marker, which he dramatically unsheathes, and writes with flair: Arnie Alliston Alum.

All the while the class still chants his name. "O.K., O.K.," says Arnie, holding up a sheaf of paper. "Somebody want to help me pass this out?" Five students jump up and Arnie distributes the handouts. Mr. Quinn retreats to one of the desks at the back. After every student has a paper, he gives Arnie a nod that he should begin. Arnie looks around, unsure how to handle the fact that Frank is still sitting on the table and that three other students put their feet up on their desks. Mr. Quinn is supportive: "You guys can be enthusiastic—and you are—but don't interfere with Arnie's work."

Arnie's work will involve teaching a class. Mr. Quinn had given the students eight options for projects to be done in conjunction with reading *Huck Finn,* and Arnie was the only one to choose the option to "Be the Teacher." Mr. Quinn is committed to giving students an opportunity to work in multiple ways and use multiple skills, and likewise, this assignment offered a range of tasks, from writing a formal literary essay to devising a cyberguide to the novel to producing a radio show or a video. Arnie's option had these instructions: "You will teach an entire class period in which you lead a discussion on a particular set of themes or some other focused topic as it relates to *Huck Finn.* During this thirty-minute period you will prepare and be ready to do the following: a) facilitate a class discussion on selected, important themes; b) introduce your lesson with some opening remarks; c) use visual aids—video clips, handouts, posters, overheads—to help the class think about and understand the ideas you present. Afterward, write a follow-up analysis of what you set out to accomplish, how well the class and you accomplished these goals, and what you learned from the whole experience."

Back to the classroom, Mr. Quinn's call for restraint works, and several students start shushing. Eric reaches over to Frank and pulls him down into his seat. The chanting stops. The class becomes quiet and Arnie looks nervous. To me the class seems unnaturally quiet, and I write in my notes, "I'm reminded of the child's verse: 'Not a creature was stirring, not even a mouse.'" Sixty-four eyes are peering up at Arnie, and it is obvious that he feels them all. Afterward, Arnie said: "It was, like, fun, cool, wow, and then, oh, my god. I'm the teacher."

"O.K., O.K.," says Arnie. "Today we're going to discuss some themes in *Huck Finn.* I came across them when I was thinking about what I wanted to share about the book. Let me read this." With the paper trembling and his voice quaking, he reads: "*Huck* has many themes. One of them is growing up. Huck not only runs away from his father, he also has to go through certain rites of passage, which will allow him to enter the adult world. Helping a slave to escape is one of these rites, since it forces Huck to make decisions about right and wrong, decisions that will determine the kind of adult he will be." He looks up and says, "That's what I want to talk about today." He glances back down at the paper. "What I'd like to do right now is this: Think about a time when you grew up in some way. A time you recall that signaled a rite of passage whether it be small or big. A time in your life you feel you matured. Then try to relate your situation to *Huck Finn.*"

Mr. Quinn nods with a satisfied grin. He and I have had many conversations about the role of literature in the high school English classroom, and I know that the design of Arnie's lesson matches Mr. Quinn's philosophy. A key principle in Mr. Quinn's classroom is that "text creates context for conversation." Huck's rites of passage became the context in which the students could consider their own journeys toward maturation.

Arnie doesn't look up when he finishes reading his sheet. Without a segue, he ploughs ahead into a story. "My example of a moment is five years ago when my father was put into prison," he says. This gets their attention. Several heads that had bobbed down snap forward like Arnie had pulled them toward him on a string. He continues:

> I believe it was a Friday, I don't remember the exact day. I was upstairs watching TV. My brother was asleep in his room, which is right next door to mine. I hear a knock on the door, and I go downstairs expecting to see someone looking for my mom or my dad or maybe one of my friends. I opened the door and there were about five or six guys in trench coats and suits. One of them said, "How are you doing?" He said, "Are your parents home?" I said, "No." Then he pulls out a badge and shows it to

me. He says, "I'm Detective so and so." I don't remember his name. He said, "We have a warrant to search the house." I was kind of, like, wondering, okay, what do I do now? . . . So, I went upstairs and woke up my brother and said, "Buddy"—that is what I call my brother—I said, "Buddy, the cops are here." He said, "What?" I said, "The cops are here." He said, "What the heck are they doing here?" So he goes downstairs and tells me to wait upstairs, and I didn't know what the heck was going on. I was wondering why the cops were here. They wouldn't let me come downstairs, and finally my mom came home and I got taken over to my uncle's house in Stanton. I didn't get told what was going on this whole time. I didn't know what the hell was the point of what they were doing. Why it was so top secret to me. It seemed like everyone else but me knew. It caused a lot of confusion. I'll never forget that day. Those moments. My brother started doing real bad things after that. So that left me alone. He started to be gone and not around. I couldn't rely on him. I also had to help my mother. Even though she takes care of me, I began to have to take care of her, and we went through a lot together. We've gone through a lot together. That was really, really tough. I had to grow up without a father. Huck has to grow up without a strong male presence in his life. That shapes him. That shapes me.

Arnie finishes and his hands disappear into the front pockets of his baggy jeans. He rocks from his heels to his toes. He looks pensive, but not embarrassed or uncertain.

"O.K., I'd like to ask people to talk about these moments. Anybody have anything to say?" he asks. He's scanning the class and people are averting their eyes. In my own teaching, I know well what I call the eternally dreadful ten seconds of wait time. Nobody moves. I'm thinking, "C'mon, c'mon somebody. Help him out. Don't let him hang." Then Arnie says, "O.K., this might be tough, but can you think of a time when you felt like you did grow up? I'd like to hear some volunteers." The hush is awkward. Arnie looks pained up there. Most students look away; some appear to be studying the fixtures. Others feign taking notes. Under the desks feet shuffle.

Above the desks there's almost no movement. It's been only about twelve seconds since Arnie asked people to share, but I'm exhausted by the tension.

"O.K., this might be tough. I guess it is tough. And maybe we could do this in small groups. Why don't we move into small groups and share?" The kids seem relieved to be moving. I feel slightly awkward and hope that a group invites me to join them, as usually happens. Today no invitation is extended, so I walk over to a group of four girls and tentatively ask if I could join them. They say, "Sure," and I squeeze into their circle. There are five of us now. These four young women are relative loners in the class. Jessie, whom I know best, Loren, Chloe, and Deb, whom I don't know at all. Jessie says, "O.K.," and then there's silence. Finally Deb says, "I have something to say." When she talks I realize it's the first time I have heard her voice. In four months I haven't heard this Asian girl either talk in class or even talk to other students. She's quiet, but it's not a shy, cowed presence. It's more of a mature detachment.

Speaking with a slight accent, pausing occasionally to find the right word, Deb offers us her story. She doesn't spill out an extended narrative but tells her story slowly, and at first hesitantly. "I grew up in Korea. I came here in the ninth grade, just three years ago. My parents are still there. They brought me here and then went back; I'm here alone. Which is really weird, but I'm getting used to it now. But it's definitely like one of those moments Arnie wanted us to talk about. My whole life sort of changed when I hit ninth grade." Jessie asks the obvious question, "Why don't your parents come here?"

For the next ten minutes we hear Deb's story of living an essentially unsupervised life in America. We begin listening with our backs pressed against the chair, but by the end we are huddled forward. Sensing our interest and perhaps our warmth, Deb opens up to us. We never get beyond her gripping story. Before Deb finishes, Arnie addresses the class. "O.K., let's head back to the big group. I've heard people talking about some vital issues. I hope that we can share some stuff now." We don't scatter. We linger. Jessie puts her hand on Deb's arm and says, "Wow, thanks for telling us that." Deb nods and seems teary. Nobody moves for another moment.

When the class is back in their seats, Arnie looks more relaxed—excited even. His decision to adjust his plan and move the class into small groups was critical to the students' comfort, and ultimately to the lesson's success. He begins, "O.K., who's gonna start?" Six hands fly up and the class steams ahead.

Combustion in the Classroom

The deepest friendships begin when we look into the eye of another and discover that they have been there, too.

—MARK NEPO, *The Book of Awakening*

In *The Grapes of Wrath,* John Steinbeck describes the fragmented lives of those streaming toward California during the Depression: "Every night a world created, complete with furniture—friends made and enemies established. Every night relationships that make a world established; and every morning the world torn down like a circus."[1] For many American teenagers, this description of worlds formed and worlds folded might sound like a typical day at school. At Stanton, students shuttle between seven different classes each day. A computer randomly assigns batches of students to each class, which meets for fifty minutes before that group breaks up and others form. One student said, "I usually have a couple of friends in each class, but mostly it's either people I don't know, or it's people whom I just barely recognize from the halls. When you ask me to distinguish between each class, it all feels like one big clump."

The students at Stanton move through their days as if on a conveyor belt. The structural impediments to forming a cohesive and enduring community are substantial; however, in the course of

the class described above, students came together to do just that.
Their experiences were marked by an elevated spirit of camaraderie,
solidarity, and mutual affection. Here are some students' responses
after Arnie's lesson:

> I thought yesterday's class was awesome. I learned so much
> about everyone. I always thought Arnie and the others were
> kind of shallow, but now they seem deeper and we all seem
> closer.

> I was, like, wow! Arnie did an excellent job. He discussed things
> well and he got the class to join in and talk about different and
> important things. He really got the class to open up. I was
> amazed! He said things that the class got to relate to, and that's
> why we all listened and talked.

> I thought Arnie's project was great. It was a way for me to get
> things off my chest and share things with my classmates. I'm
> sure he would be a great teacher or counselor.

> I think that Arnie did an amazing presentation because he raised
> an important topic and had kids share their feelings. We found
> out things about our classmates that we didn't know. I think that
> he got the students to share some of their deep inner secrets
> with the whole class and get stuff off their chests. I think it's a
> good thing to have discussions like this because people can say
> what they feel without being afraid.

> I think Arnie did a great job yesterday having us all come to-
> gether in a deep conversation. Because not only did he talk
> about the book and how Huck did this and Huck did that, but
> he was able to open up and tell us about a traumatic experience
> that happened to him, and he got the students to share experi-
> ences. The discussion was so good and deep that there was no
> pause or silent moment.

In his studies of human culture, anthropologist Victor Turner
describes simple but powerful occasions of social unity within communities. These events are not products of routine acts or choreo-

graphed rituals but "spontaneously generated relationships between leveled and equal, total and individuated human beings, stripped of structural attributes."[2] Drawing on the philosophy of Martin Buber, Turner describes the concept of *communitas* as the caring and effortless camaraderie that arises between individuals and results in an experience of connectedness "richly charged with affect."[3] Arnie's lesson clearly had this kind of effect on his classmates. As students left the room that day, Mary said, "Today's class gave me chills." Another student said, "I felt today's class in the pit of my stomach." It is worth thinking about why.

*   *   *

Classrooms are not spaces that foster deeply personal thoughts and emotions, but are regulated public arenas where sharing intimacies is usually taboo. For teachers, such personal concerns are tangential to academic objectives; for students, the environment is unsafe for revealing conversation. However, the class that Arnie taught marked the disclosure, in public, of a host of intimate issues. One student said, "I couldn't believe how honest people were being with their most private, hidden stuff. At first, I was, like, hold on—this is English class. What's going on?" Mr. Quinn was also touched by the depth of the conversation. He said, "What made that so compelling was that Arnie's sharing was so honest. He's not a guy who's done the therapy game. He's not used to talking about himself like that. But he did. And so did Kyle and Jason. Those guys don't open up like that often, anywhere."

I asked Arnie why he decided to share such a raw and personal story. He told me that he had agonized over the decision and had talked it over with his mother, but he also said that he hadn't planned on telling the whole story. "I told the story of my father being in jail at the beginning, but I hadn't planned on explaining why he was in jail. Then it just sort of came out." He decided to divulge parts of the story because it "felt right at the time." Indeed, Turner discusses the spontaneous nature of some forms of community, specifically, those that come about because they transgress the norms that govern conventional ways of interacting within an organization. For Turner, it is the dissolution of strictures that catalyzes the experience of what he calls "unprecedented potency."[4]

I also asked Arnie if while he was teaching he felt that something special might be happening. Arnie was reminded of Vincent's story of how his father left his family a year ago. "I think I felt something working a little bit into Vincent's discussion or viewpoint. I don't know exactly what you would call it. I just looked around and noticed the class, and everybody was focused on him. There was no side conversation; there was no jittering, or anybody doing homework. All eyes were on him. Everything was focused on him. And I, I kind of clicked, and I knew this was working and I had come up with what was a powerful idea."

Here's how it went: Vincent, a gritty kid and a celebrated athlete, openly dabs a tear from his eye while he's talking. He tells us, "My mom was crushed when my dad left, and then my sister started taking drugs, and I sort of felt the tons getting piled onto my back. I needed to be strong and be grown up. I wasn't used to being like that." When Vincent has finished his story, Arnie gives him a look of such compassion, such fraternal tenderness that I feel myself choking up. Arnie then says, "That kind of sucks. It's always somebody around our age that has to take on the stuff. It always seems to fall to our age group to hold things together."

It's now silent. Arnie's eyes rest on Vincent, who's looking down at his desk. Rosie leans over and affectionately puts her hand on his back and leaves it there. After a few seconds, Mr. Quinn speaks. It's the first time he's said anything since he intervened at the beginning of class to temper the kids' good-natured cheering. "Nowadays, teenagers have to shoulder a lot more than they used to." Oddly, Mr. Quinn's adult voice sounds out of place.

Lilia, who is sitting at the front of the room, starts to talk. She's not looking at the class but is staring straight ahead, her hair covering her face. "My brother, you know, he's been diagnosed with cancer. I don't really ever talk about it, but it's big. My dad's not really around and that's forced me to grow up. It's not an option—it's not an option—not growing up when something like this happens."

Vincent, with Jessica's arm still across his back, says in a grave voice, "I don't know." He's shaking his head, "I don't know about our age, sixteen- to eighteen-year-olds. Maybe it's good that things happen to us. You know, the problems come to us and we handle them, and then maybe we learn how to handle them."

Arnie leans against Mr. Quinn's lectern and nods his head. "I think problems are happening all the time—since we're born—and our parents do their best to hide it from us." Jason adds, "Maybe part of growing up is that we've gotten better at picking up stuff that our parents used to hide from us. Like we're smarter now or something."

Arnie moves off the lectern. "My mom tried so hard to hide stuff from us. I didn't say this before, but my father was accused of sexual molestation. I didn't know that was why he first went away, but I started to notice things like why my aunt didn't come over and why my mother didn't hang around with her sister anymore."

I look around the room and students are craning toward Arnie. Often students lean breezily back in their seats, but not today. The tenor and pace of the class were different, too. Sometimes class discussions are characterized by adolescent verbal banter where the goal is to be funny or impress Mr. Quinn. Today, however, students took turns, often leaving tracts of respectful silence.

That day, the kids in Mr. Quinn's class spent an hour talking about life, death, rites of passage, friendship, and love, all in the context of thinking about what made them grow. Together, they wrestled with the unanswerable questions fundamental to all of us. These issues fill the pages of our greatest literature and are the focus of our most memorable conversations, yet we know they rarely reach our classrooms.

The students' stories contain themes that are at the heart of the adolescent world. Yet schools seem to keep the heart at bay. I asked Mary if she has had many conversations like the one the class had that day. "No," she answered. "We talk about things like who the character in the book is or what the formula for the cube is. We don't talk about how we feel about important issues." And when I interviewed Trey a year later, he said this about his senior year English class: "We started reading *Hamlet* two fucking months ago. So I rented the movie because the Shakespeare stuff is tough. And the movie was great. Mel Gibson's a bad dude. The movie is about passion and hate. I don't know what the hell we've been talking about for the last six weeks because it's not about those things when we read it in class."

Trey's observation is telling. The white-hot themes of passion, hate, love, and sex were cooled to lukewarm for the adolescent audience. That which was rich and colorful was rendered flat and bland. The problem, however, is that adolescents need opportunities for deep conversation. The developmental turbulence of adolescence requires it. To ignore this need squanders a growing mind's vitality and curiosity.

Twenty-eight of the thirty-two students participated publicly in the conversation. This was the highest percentage of participation that I witnessed all year. The conversation mattered to students, and they responded by taking the risk to open up to their classmates. For example, Tristan, a reserved and shy young woman, talked unsolicited for the only time all year. She offered the class her story of how her father had left her mother and how she's had to become her mother's best friend to support her. Afterward she said, "I sometimes sit there and get angry. I always look out at other girls and think, that bitch has it easier than I do, but I guess I learned how much everybody is dealing with. That's what I'll remember." Mia shared a similar set of thoughts. "I mean I used to look at Arnie and think he's this muscle-bound, pompous ass. I mean, I think, 'Oh, there's Mr. Popularity.' But after hearing him and Jason and Vincent and Tristan, I realize there's more to them. Just like there's more to me."

Mia suggests that this conversation made an enduring impact on the class. What happened that day mattered to students, and as educational researcher Arthur Applebee writes in *Curriculum as Conversation,* we should be teaching a "curriculum that matters."[5] He defines this kind of curriculum as one that addresses knowledge that is important to individuals and to society. I heard students say this in various ways throughout the year. They wanted to have heartfelt conversations in their classrooms and with their teachers. They believed that as maturing young people they needed space and time to discuss issues pertinent to their lives. Again, Arnie said it best: "I think that Huck growing up teaches a lot about our own growing up. We need to have intelligent conversations like this in our classes. That's what pushed me to do this lesson the way I did. I mean we've had intelligent conversations before about important stuff with Mr. Quinn, and I felt and hoped that we could do it again."

Cultivating Community in the Classroom

In my analysis of this classroom episode I focus on two pivotal factors. First, I examine how Mr. Quinn designs and carries out a curriculum that features a successful transaction between the canon and the personal. Second, I look at how this episode provided a distinct and unusual forum for the students' perspective to assume a featured role.

Evoking the Personal

Most high school teachers would agree that literature can be a catalyst to stir connections in and give meaning to students' own lives, but this rarely happens. Arnie's lesson, however, fulfilled the promise of a class where, as Mr. Quinn has often said, the text created the context for conversation. Arnie was the catalyst that stirred the connectedness, but the culture of Mr. Quinn's classroom fostered the conditions that supported Arnie's efforts.

The library in Mr. Quinn's classroom—his canonical stash—locates his work in the larger traditions of his discipline. The big stories of the literary canon and the little stories of personal experience work as complementary partners in his class. Educator Parker J. Palmer writes beautifully of trying to fashion a classroom where this partnership thrives.

> A learning space should not be filled with abstractions so bloated that no room remains for the small but soulful realities that grow in our students' lives. In this space there must be ample room for the little stories of individuals, stories of personal experience in which the student's inner teacher is at work. But when my little story, or yours, is our only point of reference, we easily become lost in narcissism. So the big stories of the discipline must also be told in the learning space—stories that are universal in scope and archetypal in depth, that frame our personal tales and help us understand what they mean. We must help students learn to listen to the big stories with the same respect we accord individuals when they tell us the tales of their lives.[6]

Arnie intended his lesson to become a conversation between the students and the text of *Huck Finn*. He instructed his classmates to think about a time in their lives when they felt they matured and relate it back to the novel. Arnie based the design of his lesson on Mr. Quinn's model: "I tried to do what Mr. Quinn and other good teachers do. They make me see my life in a book. That's what happened to me when I read *Huck* anyway."

Fashioning meaningful conversations between text and students is a core feature of Mr. Quinn's pedagogy. For example, a week before Arnie's lesson, Mr. Quinn asked students to create a mandala using *Huck Finn* and their own lives as source material. Mandalas are symbolic representations of magic circles, and the center usually holds an essential symbol or truth. Stories or visions become symbolized through connections to the center. These are the directions he gave the class: "The center circle should contain what you feel are the different stages of life through which we all pass. You should include the characteristics of each stage (e.g., if you say "adolescence" is a stage, then what are the distinguishing features of that stage of life?). The second circle should include those stages of life as applied to *Huck Finn;* for example, which stage is Huck at in the book; and where is Jim? What about Miss Watson or Aunt Polly? Judge Thatcher? Provide examples that illustrate why they are at that stage. The last circle outlines your own life: identify the stages you have already gone through and what they were like; then identify those stages you will go through and what will happen in those stages, what they will be like."

This assignment generated uniformly provocative responses. Students, for example, talked about parents who reminded them of Pap and the conflicts of seeking independence as a teenager. The task was designed to demonstrate the instructive potential of literature in life. As he told students when introducing the assignment, "A few years ago I was reading *Hamlet* to a group of seniors, and I came to the point where Hamlet accused his mother of a relationship with his uncle. At the time I was teaching this, my own father had died. I was still working through a lot of that stuff, and now my mother was dating the old football coach at my high school. In the middle of class, I just stopped and said, 'I can't handle this right now. I can't go on.' I was really moved, powerfully moved, by Shakespeare entering a space, a raw space, in my life. Listen to how literature can inform your life. That's what this mandala is asking."

By inviting the stories of our lives to dance with the stories of our traditions we have to be prepared to be open and vulnerable. Mr. Quinn navigates these waters when he shares glimpses of his own life, and he accepts the risk attached to it. He values intimate expression and uses it to steer the class. This is the ethos that allowed the class to move into rare terrain during Arnie's lesson.

One of the things I wondered while I was watching Arnie share his story was how he knew that he would be able to say all that in front of the class. He explained:

> I thought about a lot. Even the night before I was thinking: 'Do I really want to share this?' I told my mom about what I was planning on doing and she said: 'Are you sure you want to talk about his? Are you going to feel comfortable?' I told her, 'If you were in my English class you'd understand.' There are a lot of good people in here and I feel that Mr. Q. does the same thing himself. He opened up to us. He's told me and us about incidents before in the past with friends and problems and about himself. Other kids have shared stuff too because we have those kinds of talks. It kind of got me inspired, too. I wasn't afraid to share anything. You know he's done the same and nobody's said anything to him, and we've had thoughtful conversations because we can talk like this.

Mr. Quinn provided the pedagogical model, but Arnie's plan for only student-centered conversation also contributed to this lesson's success. Lilia, the student who shared the story of her brother's cancer, said, "I love conversations. I love discussion, but it so rarely happens in a real way. I wish we had more time to talk. But the teachers like to talk and they are the ones who are in charge. It felt good to say what I said because of the way the class handled me."

When the Kids Take Charge of the Conversation

Educational research shows that most verbal exchange in the classroom adheres to formulaic question-and-answer routines, often called the recitation model.[7] Classroom talk typically follows a three-part sequence of teacher initiation, student response, and teacher evaluation (IRE), where teachers control the topic, the sequence of whose turn it is, and the reward system. This classroom episode that we've examined deviates from this structure in several ways.

First, Mr. Quinn retreats to the background. In a typical discussion he is a forceful presence, taking nearly half of the turns. Research on secondary classroom discussion indicates that this percentage is at the lower end of the spectrum; most teachers dominate the class with nearly three-fourths of the turns in a discussion.[8] In this class discussion, Mr. Quinn made only four comments where there were more than eighty turns taken.

More important than the quantity of turns, even, are the kinds of contributions Mr. Quinn made. An excerpt from my notes describes one of them:

> Jerry is still holding the left side of his chest as he finishes his story about being stabbed last year while he lived in San Jose and was in a Latino gang. He's shared a gripping story. "Now that I've moved here, I'm trying to be better. I made an agreement with my Dad and I want to hold it, to keep it. Now I stick to myself. That's why you don't see me talk to people in class or in the hall. I started going to tae kwan do and that helps me think about virtue and being good. It helps me think about the way I want to be and then it teaches me to act the way I want to be." Again, silence answers. I watch Mr. Quinn. Sitting as a student,

he lifts his hand once and then hesitantly puts it down. He puts it up hesitantly, drops it again, and makes a sound—"T-t-t." Then he stops and puts his hand up. Arnie notices him and says, "Mr. Quinn?" Mr. Quinn says, "Thank you, Jerry, for sharing that. I'm sitting here thinking about one of the things that really stands out to me. Something that I haven't thought about is how much of adolescence is figuring out relationships with each other. What does it mean to have an agreement and relationship with your dad? I guess it's not just adolescence: What does it mean for me to have to a relationship with my mother?" He pauses. "You know, that's one of things that Mark Twain figured out. I think that is part of Twain's brilliance. He highlights the chinks in the armor of adults. We expect adults to have the answer but he gives us a world where adults are the ones doing the bad stuff." Arnie nods his head and then says, "Thanks, Mr. Quinn. Now, going back to what Jerry said."

This sequence highlights several important features of Mr. Quinn's contributions. First, he attempts to participate as an actual student. He chooses not to usurp Arnie's role and break into the conversation. He raises his hand and restrains himself, waiting for Arnie to acknowledge him. His actions publicly honor the legitimacy of Arnie's work. Also, his contribution is conversant rather than didactic. He affirms rather than offering a summary judgment.

In the past, though, I had seen Mr. Quinn respond to a student story with a judgment. For example, a few days before, during a discussion about what Pap taught Huck about morality, Tristan said, "I know what it is like when a parent holds a belief system that you might find wrong. My dad sometimes says things that I disagree with and I don't know what to do." Tristan paused for a second, and it seemed that she was going to explain something more, but Mr. Quinn jumped in and said, "Thanks, Tristan, for sharing that important thought. It's exactly what we're getting at. It helps us think about conflicts with parents around values and ethics. We all face this." Tristan nodded and Mr. Quinn moved on. This example illustrates the difference in his response to Jerry's story; he affirmed rather than evaluated.

I asked Mr. Quinn about his comment during Jerry's conversation. He was keenly aware of trying to collaborate in Arnie's lesson but at the same time nudge it toward important outcomes. He described his experience: "The reason I kept withdrawing my hand was because I didn't want to interrupt, but I felt like I needed to participate. I was undecided, but then some of the things being said felt almost scary and dangerous. I needed to pose some questions and frame what was being said in a way that let us explore it differently. . . . I was also helping us follow deeper into the connections between growing up and *Huck Finn*. Mostly, I wanted to recognize that what Jerry said was heavy, and I wanted him to know that I heard him."

Mr. Quinn also recognized that what was accomplished in this class was special. Afterward we sat down together, and I asked him what he thought. He leaned his head back, exhaled, and held out his arm. "I think the hair is still standing up." He continued, "I don't think I could have achieved that conversation today. I maybe could have, but it would have been . . . I don't think it could have been like that. I think it was because a student was saying let's talk about some things that are important. Arnie had access to them in a way that I don't know if I can get. What he did was establish a rare conversational space."

In modeling his personal connection to *Huck Finn*, Arnie set in motion powerful forces. He shared his story and his pain in a way that made this strapping young man seem enormously vulnerable and fragile. He set the precedent for what would follow. As a student with significant social status and influence, he was respected by his peers for his candor; they saw it as an act of courage. They honored him by treating his story with kindness, respect, and reciprocity. He knew this. I asked him later that day what stood out for him about the class he taught. He said, "Today we had a discussion that was open. That's what I think I'll remember most about it was its openness. People were *actually thinking*, our work was our thinking. What makes this class stand out is that we can all relate to each other. We care . . . wait, I don't want to say that. It's too important a word to use about everybody in the class, but we all respect each other, and when you show respect, you'll get respect back. I'm just really grateful for the people in the class, because we can't have a discussion like that without the students wanting to. We really came together."

Yes they did. And the result was an indelible and luminous moment—for all of us.

CHAPTER 5

Grasping Insight
An Episode of Coming to Know Yourself

Sylvia Plath's poem "Mirror" describes a moment of stark self-appraisal:

> I am silver and exact.
> I have no preconceptions.
> Whatever I see I swallow immediately
> Just as it is, unmisted by love or dislike.
> I am not cruel, only truthful—
> The eye of a little god, four-cornered.

Plath's mirror reflects back an "exact" chronicle of the self without "preconception." It's "unmisted" and "only truthful." Seeing yourself with new clarity is a compelling but elusive encounter, and it is one that has been written about for ages. Socrates gave us the deceptively simple maxim: "Know thyself." Heidegger identified *die Lichtung,* or clearing, where one experiences a potent truth by grasping reality.

Encounters with the self can be both harrowing and transfixing, particularly for young people searching for identity. Apprehending a truth about our life can be fraught with peril and pain, so we often build elaborate layers of insulation. John W. Gardner observes that "human beings have always employed an enormous variety of clever devices for running away from themselves, and the modern world is particularly rich in such stratagems."[1] We're fugitives from our selves, and we carefully avoid direct encounters with Plath's mirror. "We can keep ourselves so busy, fill our lives with so many diversions, stuff our heads with so much knowledge, involve ourselves with so many people and cover so much ground that we never have time to probe the fearful and wonderful world within."[2]

In this chapter I tell the story of how one class gained insight into their way of being in the world. They experienced what Michael Polyani writes about as "comprehending," or the "grasping of disjointed parts into a comprehensive whole" that is "manifestly personal."[3]

These episodes of understanding can be particularly powerful for a young person. Given the rapid pace of inner and outer change during adolescence, moments of comprehension can be moments of experiencing a hard and penetrating truth.

> As the young move, . . . horizons are breached; the landscape is transformed; experiences are clarified.
>
> —MAXINE GREENE, *Releasing the Imagination*

Class begins with a flurry of questions about the upcoming presentations. Mr. Quinn responds to each one with variations of "Thank you, that's a good question" or "I hadn't thought about that yet." His speech, his expressions, even his physical stance assure the young people that he takes them seriously. After the last question he tells the students what's in store for the day. "I have these two poems which I came across that have much to offer us in thinking about the qualities of the 'American mind.' I want you to read these poems and then respond to them in writing. So take out a piece of paper and get ready. You know, I want you to hear these poems. It's important to hear them. Let me read them. Do you know Marge Piercy? She's one of my favorite poets."

He distributes copies of the poems and reads. "This poem is called 'Barbie Doll.'"

This girlchild was born as usual
and presented dolls that did pee-pee
and miniature GE stoves and irons
and wee lipsticks the color of cherry candy.
Then in the magic of puberty, a classmate said:
You have a great big nose and fat legs.

She was healthy, tested intelligent,
possessed strong arms and back,
abundant sexual drive and manual dexterity
She went to and fro apologizing.
Everyone saw a fat nose on thick legs.

She was advised to play coy,
exhorted to come on hearty,
exercise, diet, smile and wheedle.
Her good nature wore out
like a fan belt.
So she cut off her nose and her legs
and offered them up.

In the casket displayed on satin she lay
with the undertaker's cosmetics painted on,
a turned-up putty nose,
dressed in a pink and white nightie.

Doesn't she look pretty? everyone said,
Consummation at last.
To every woman a happy ending.

To say that he read the poem undercharacterizes the event. He performed the poem. He paused after the line, "Then in the magic of puberty, a classmate said," and then in a voice dripping with juvenile cruelty, he read "You have a great big nose and fat legs." As he paces and reads, I hear his feet shuffle and the coins jangle in his pocket. It is testimony to the quiet that these soft sounds are perceptible. I see Loren shaking her head back and forth. Mary stares at her ring, turning it around and around. Mr. Quinn looks out at the class, asking for reactions. Frank blurts out, "I don't get it." William sighs,

"C'mon Frank, it just means that you don't get plastic surgery." The jocks in the room crack up. Mia throws them a sneer. I hear Loren mouth "Assholes."

Mr. Quinn approaches the boys' cluster of desks. "No," he says, his voice brittle. "It is about respect." Each syllable is punctuated with his glare. The boys seem ashamed; Arnie and William both tell me later that in fact they felt terrible.

Mr. Quinn speaks, his voice still clipped. "Let's look at the next poem. It's by Langston Hughes, and it's called 'Theme for English B.'"

His reading sounds strained. He finishes and assigns a task. "Please respond to one of the poems. What does the poem say to you? What does it say about the 'American mind?'"

Making Sense of Yourself

Engrossment in thought has discernible, observable qualities. Loren's eyes bore into the photocopied page. A furrow creases her forehead as she underlines some lines, writes a few words, and darts her eyes to the poem. Mary leans on her elbow, gnawing on her pen. Mia spins the inner hoop of an earring while silently mouthing the poem and writing in bursts. Neil, who is Loren's neighbor, braids the hairs of his sparse goatee; his other finger traces the lines on the poem. The young women in the class seem particularly focused. After a span Mr. Quinn asks the class to turn in the papers. Five boys move to the front.

Jeff and Loren often exchange papers during these writing assignments. Jeff asks her now, "Which didja write about?" Jeff pushes Loren his paper and moves for hers. It's normally a routine exchange, but this time Loren clutches her paper to her chest. Jeff looks startled and says, "Sorry."

Loren continues to write. "This poem is about how a person can say something to someone without thinking and hurt them very easily. You say something not meaning to hurt, but that person is thinking that it's true and eagerly goes and changes themselves. This poem reminds me of me."

In Edward Hirsch's book *How to Read a Poem* he describes the relationship between a poet, the poem, and the reader as a dynamic relational process. He likens a poem to stored magic. "The reader completes a poem, and in the process brings to it his or her own past experiences. You are reading poetry—I mean really reading it when you feel encountered and changed by a poem, when you feel its seismic vibrations, the sounding of your depth."[4]

Jen had exactly this kind of response. "This poem was written when I was two, and yet I feel like it was written to me. At the end of everyday I go home and feel like cutting off every part William, C.J., and Vaughn ridiculed today. Yet I don't. I know that's letting them win. To me this is my poem. It helps me understand myself, those guys, and lots of other things. Seeing something like that makes you realize a lot of things about how I've acted around guys, and it also makes me want to change things."

Mia, scorning the jocks in the class, told me, "Those guys are such idiots. They're just like, it's about some stupid girl who can't handle life, and I'm, like, sitting there thinking, 'No, it's about how people treat other people and how they can't respect another person's difference.' That poem's about me, and they acted that poem out. They made those words come true. They did today just what she wrote about. They made that poem reality."

On Monday Mia walked into class and handed me a poem called "Barbie Doll and Me." She had shared other reflections with me during the year, but this was the first in the form of a poem.

> He said, "Listen to this and tell me what you think."
> I listened to it, missing the link
> But upon hearing it, I felt my heart sink

A tale of a girl who couldn't laugh
a sorrowful, but Beautiful epitaph
and in the room there was a laugh
Soon I could clearly see
that girl was just like me
her future was meant for me
But unlike her, I won't let them win
Because to me that's a mortal sin
and I'm not desperate to be let in
My eyes pierce their soul
but all that's there is a big hole
the emptiness will never be full
I used to listen, like her, but no more
They'll come to me, I'll slam the door
useless boys looking to score
They cry out, "I am great"
but can see the terrible fate
They'll say "I'm sorry" but it'll be too late
because that Barbie is dead
she cut her nose off her head
when she could have fought instead.
So to her I dedicate this poem
and I know I'm not alone.

Mia identified with the girl in the poem. She told me, "I'm like most girls at Stanton in that we heed all the commandments of how we're supposed to dress and be beautiful. What we're supposed to wear and smell like. I used to think that I thought for myself, but we aren't really thinking for ourselves. That's what I mean when I say in the poem that it is our beautiful epitaph. It's about almost all the girls here. We're so occupied with what they think."

Mary said, "I think Barbies are toys that most girls grow up playing with. I did have a lot of fun playing with my Barbies. I also remember how I started to play with Barbie, and then try and copy how my Barbie was dressed, and then I tried to do my makeup like Barbie. This was all when I was a little kid. . . . I realize now that Barbie is just what starts little girls believing they have to be perfect.

Jen said, "It was like Mr. Quinn coached those boys so that we would really get the poem."

One of the Asian students wrote, "Being an American is tough. We have this certain image that people expect. This poem makes me realize even more that when you're not born with the beige skin, blond hair, blue eyes, you are not considered important."

Encounters with art can shake us up. In *The Act of Reading: A Theory of Aesthetic Response,* Wolfgang Iser contends that our horizons are broadened when we interpret a text. "The literary text enables its readers to transcend the limitations of their own real-life situation; it is not a reflection of any given reality, but it is an extension or broadening of their own reality."[5] After reading the poem, Mia said, "The poem gives me language and an idea to understand things I feel and do. I'm not proud that I have a little Barbie in me." Every one of the young women in class that day suggested either in writing or in an interview that this poem clarified how the world they lived in burdens them with expectations of beauty. Many of their comments echoed Mary's: "I guess I knew about expectations for beauty and stuff, but this cleared it up for me. I don't know if it's a big deal, but I slept in yesterday instead of getting up and getting makeup on." When I asked her if that resulted from the poem, she said: "Yeah, I guess. I don't know how long it will last though."

The poem Mr. Quinn read didn't apply to only the young women in the class. Jason said, "This first poem was very brutal. It made me realize something. . . . As a child my step-aunt was always being made fun of. She was overweight and was not well liked. Because of the teasing, she became bulimic. She lost over eighty pounds and became weak and frail. She was forced to enter a hospital. . . . She died at the age of thirty because of bulimia. It had weakened her heart. I guess that's what can happen when we don't think about what we say."

Edgar said he was moved not so much by the poem but by how

the girls in the class responded to it. "I watched them, and I could see them all thinking, 'That's me.' or, 'Yeah, I do that.' And then William made that stupid joke. I thought Mary was going to either cry or hit him. It's weird. I like to see beautiful girls. I like to see them dress up and look nice. I never think about what it means to be them. I tell you what, I'm damn glad I'm a man. It would be tough."

Teenagers yearn to make sense of their world, and this poem helped some kids understand something important in it. A few of the young women found this experience empowering. Jen said, "I like things that make me see the world clearer and differently, I feel powerful after that." Mia writes of planning to "pierce their soul," "slam the door," and "fight instead." Another said that young women need to "fight against those tendencies we have. The poem gives a great message." One student put the poem next to her mirror to remind herself that "she can be strong." There were other times during the year when a lesson in class gave the students a lesson in life. For example, several classes were devoted to talking about Nathan McCall's autobiography, *Makes Me Wanna Holler.* The book details McCall's rollercoaster rise from a violent, misogynistic gang member to a *Washington Post* reporter.[6] Discussions that ensued centered on what one of the students called "strong topics"—including racism, substance abuse, and treatment of woman. Many students, particularly the young men, later described these conversations as the most compelling of the year. Vincent said: "Sometimes I'd walk out of class after one of these strong-topic conversations, and I couldn't stop thinking about it. I'd start talking about it with my friends. We have this class before lunch, and I'd be having lunch with them, and they'd say, 'I'm not racist or nothing.' And I'd be, like, that's bullshit and tell 'em about something that happened in McCall's book, and they'd be, like, 'Wow, maybe you're right.' "

I asked him later why he thought he continued the conversation after class. "These topics get into your personal life. You understand a problem in a way that you didn't, and you're, like, heck, I can do something about that. And then you do." Transformative educator Paulo Freire understands these events as a "naming of the world."[7] Freire believes that we gain dignity and hope when we unsilence the world and listen to its workings. He writes, "To exist, humanly, is to *name* the world, to change it. Once named, the world in its turn reappears to the namers as a problem and requires of them a new *naming*. . . . If it is in speaking their word that people, by naming the world transform it, dialogue imposes itself as the way by which they achieve significance as human beings."[8]

Cultivating an Episode of Self-Understanding

One of the reasons that episodes of personal understanding are rare in the classroom is that they are elusive in life. Yet when they do occur, they can be pivotal to a person's sense of self. In this section I discuss why these moments may be difficult to design. I then examine how the content and tone of Piercy's poem, as well as Mr. Quinn's reading of it, worked to capture the students' interest.

Potent Poetry: The Role of Curriculum

A curious and pervasive irony of the typical high school English classroom is the contrast between the richness of the literature and the flaccidity of the student-teacher encounter with that material. The core curriculum in most high school English classes includes texts rich with meaning, yet most classroom interaction about these works centers on the production of referential meanings: recall of story events, comprehension of plot structures, and identification of literary devices.[9] So although most high school study of literature involves relatively low-level processes of comprehension, this kind of learning does not uncover the meaty complexity of a text, which lies in asking what it means.

Literature seeks to express the intricacies and uncertainties of human experience. When done well, Martha Nussbaum tells us, the writer's art acts like "winged creatures piercing where the blunt terms of ordinary speech or of abstract theoretical discourse are blind, acute where they are obtuse, winged where they are dull and heavy."[10] Piercy's poem becomes for the students a piercing winged creature. Arnie said: "I know that our words can hurt people. I know that, but when you read a poem where this woman cuts off her nose because of words, you see it more powerfully. . . . That's the power of reading that."

The poem invites attention from students because it redefines a simultaneously adored and jeered icon of American youth. The text is replete with inversions: it begins with an idyllic retrospective of perky dolls and "wee lipsticks," but then the "magic of puberty" transforms the perfect curves of Barbie into a "great big nose and fat legs." Lydia wrote, "I never thought of my Barbie like that." Edgar said, "I'm going to go home, and trash my little sister's Barbies." The way Piercy addresses the poem's audience also captured the class's attention. "When the poem began with talking about pee-pee and cherry candy lipstick, I thought I was listening to Oprah—not a poem," said Linda. Piercy's tone is informal and sounds more chatty than academic. It struck me that the two texts least enjoyed by the class during the year were *The Scarlet Letter* and *Cannery Row.* Students expressed frustration with the tone and impenetrable language in the books. As one student said, "Did I like *The Scarlet Letter?* Hell, no, I could barely understand what the characters were freaking saying."[11]

The poem's content draws the students in, with issues of beauty, sexuality, death, cruelty, and acceptance. It conveys moral outrage by inverting the image of Barbie from light to dark, from simple to complex, from safe to lethal. Loren, the captain of the cheerleading team, said that the poem made her rethink her relationship with Barbie. She wrote, "Barbie's everyone's idol when you're young. Every little girl's fantasies are lived out through Barbie. She has the man, the clothes, the money, and the car. Let's just face it, the girl has everything! But then you read this and it's different. It makes you think."

The provocative text steers close to taboo terrain. Its references to "sexual drive" and the "magic of puberty" hit hard against classroom boundaries. The students sense this and respond. Classrooms have long been indicted for undertreating the existential, sexual, and moral questions of adolescence.[12] Mia told me, "We never read stuff about real life. It's always sugar-coated. It's always reading about 'I hear America singing' or about grown-ups who feel bad about grown-up problems. This is the cruel but real stuff. This is my world." Andre said something similar, "We don't usually talk about these things. It kind of goes unsaid, but it's the reality. I try not to hurt people, but people hurt everybody all the time. I see it—that's why it's good to talk about this and to read this."

I believe that another reason that this class episode was so successful was that it allowed students to consider a moral question. As Vincent said, "We're dying to talk about stuff that's important. It's just that we rarely have opportunity to do that in most classes." The preponderance of evidence about American education suggests that we rarely consider moral issues in the classroom in ways that matter deeply to students. One of the more convincing studies on the reluctance of teachers and students to engage forcefully with moral and existential issues is found in Kathy Simon's book *Moral Questions in the Classroom*. Simon found that despite the frequent emergence of these issues in everyday classroom discussions, they are most often ignored or shut down.[13]

This poem invited students to participate in a conversation that mattered to them.

Performing: The Role of Mr. Quinn

One student summed up his reaction to most poetry with: "It doesn't make a bit of fucking sense when I read it." Poetry can be difficult for students when it compresses and redefines language into forms that seem impenetrable. Even in Mr. Quinn's class, lessons that involved poetry had a tortured reputation. Why was Piercy's poem received differently?

One explanation points to the multisensory encounter students have with "Barbie Doll." Poetry is both a statement and a song. Poet and teacher Kenneth Koch writes that "in reading prose or in hearing people talk we aren't much aware of anything resembling music. There are no horns, no piano, no strings, no drums."[14] Mr. Quinn's dramatic reading of the poem, however, made it accessible as music. Koch writes about the "beauty and grace of the words that are hauling in the meaning so that we have to respond to it both as music and as sense." And students responded because they are open and receptive to issues they wonder about. They struggle to understand such great themes as power, beauty, intimacy, weakness, cruelty, and love. These issues raise their hackles.

Mr. Quinn also got the class's interest by bringing the poem on his own initiative to the curriculum. Students railed against those teachers who taught solely "by the book." As one student told me, "I hate social studies; he teaches straight out of the book." Another said, "There's nothing worse than just following the book and the curriculum, day after day, class after class. It gets numbing." Yet another said, "What I hate is a teacher who just mechanically follows what is in the textbook and then gives worksheets so that we can do the test. Mr. Quinn makes stuff up for us so that we find it interesting." Students were grateful for Mr. Quinn's efforts to customize their education rather than following some inflexible master plan. Students knew that Mr. Quinn treated them as worthy partners in an intellectual discourse. As he said in his introduction to the class that day that Marge Piercy is "one of *my* favorite poets." Maybe now she'll be one of theirs, too.

CHAPTER 6

Doing Good
An Episode of Enacting Virtue

You know, it feels good to do good.
—KOBEY, age sixteen

When our actions mesh with our vision of good and we leave a positive imprint on others, we feel noble and powerful. We relish moments when our conduct in the world aligns with our concept of what we hope to be. This congruence between what we know and what we do can be inspiring for teenagers figuring their way in the world.

In this chapter I describe a yearlong community service project organized by Mr. Quinn. Each week a group of high school students visited a kindergarten class at the Kennedy Elementary School, where the teenagers read stories to the children. The experience resonated with adolescents because they believed that they were doing good. "We made the world a better place," said one volunteer. In particular I address the class's efforts at the end of the year to write a grant to raise money for books for each of the kindergartners.

A Portrait of Doing Good

The group parades across the school's parking lot and heads down one of Stanton's sedate, tree-canopied streets. Arnie, Trey, and several other boys have the lead. A middle-aged woman sees them and clutches her purse. We troop past a playground, and a group of toddlers stares. Students wave at the little ones, who lift brightly colored rakes and shovels back at us. The class is heading off to Kennedy Elementary School to culminate what Mr. Quinn called the "mother of all school projects."

The project began early in the school year at the behest of Mrs. Smith, the service-learning coordinator at Stanton, who had been seeking teacher volunteers for new classroom-based community service projects. Mr. Quinn offered to participate, though in early October he said, "I really have no expectations of this Kennedy thing. Right now I release three to five kids each Friday from class, and they head over to Kennedy to read to kindergartners. I think the students like it, but right now it operates as this stand-alone satellite project that I support on the principle that some of my most reluctant, cranky readers are going off to read."

As the year progressed, it became clear to Mr. Quinn that these students were having, in his words, a "magical experience." "Something special is happening between these kids and the kindergartners. They return glowing." Mr. Quinn's sense of the educative magic at work was confirmed by many student testimonials.

Rhonda, for example, said, "I came into the class second semester, but I had heard about the reading experience, and I was anxious to try it—although I was a little scared, too. I remember the first time I went to Kennedy, I walked in the door, and three girls just ran up to me and grabbed me. They were pulling me by my hand to the library, they were so anxious for me to read to them. That made me feel so good." And Jeannie said, "Every Friday I went I felt great. I mean it's so much fun to sit there with the kids and read, but this week I went and took the students to the library to pick out some books, and I noticed this little girl looking through the stacks. All of a sudden she pulls out this book and marches over with a big grin and hands me the book—it was the book that we had read last week. She gives me a serious face and says, 'I'm going to read this one *all by myself.*' I know she couldn't read, but she wanted to read the book that I had introduced to her. It was the cutest thing I ever saw. I felt so good after that. I felt like I was helping these kids care about reading and that I was helping them look at reading with a good attitude."

As the year progressed, students became more passionate about the experience. Every Tuesday Mr. Quinn would ask which students would like to spend Friday at Kennedy. Early in the year the hands were sporadic and he would ask, "Anybody else? Anybody else who hasn't gone yet?" By midyear, more than twenty hands shot up.

In March Billy and Mr. Quinn had a conversation that seren-dipitously transformed the modest goals of the project to something significantly more ambitious. During a unit on comma usage, Mr. Quinn shared a story about how important writing is in his own life. He explained why mastering the conventions of grammar shouldn't be underestimated. He told them, "Writing forcefully and well can help you leverage many opportunities. Last week, I wrote a grant for an elementary school. Because I was able to represent their perspec-tive in writing, I can help them find funding sources. In other words, writing well can provide you with earning potential and, in many ways, power."

After this explanation, Billy calls out, "Hey, we should do that for our kids at Kennedy." Mr. Quinn initially doesn't respond, but after several moments he looks intensely at Billy and says, "Hey, hey, that's a terrific idea. That's a really promising idea." Billy continues, "We could give each kid a book, which would be cool." Mr. Quinn begins to look excited. "Come to think about it, that's a terrific idea. My son Lowell had this experience where a fourth grader would come to his kindergarten class to read to him. I couldn't believe how excited he would get about this older kid coming to read to him. At the end of the year he got this book, and he literally slept with the book. We couldn't tear him loose from it. If you guys were to give books to those kids, it would make an impact." Billy is clearly ignited by the possibilities. "Yeah, we could do that. I know those kids would think it's awesome." Jen adds, "I bet the teachers would be so grateful. One of them was saying that she couldn't believe how few of her students actually have books at home and read with their parents."

A plan emerges to write a grant soliciting funds from companies, bookstores, and local philanthropic foundations to buy books for the children. Ten students volunteer to spearhead the grant writing. These students meet over several months to strategize, write, send out queries, meet with foundation officers, and order books. Mr. Quinn serves as a one-person advisory board overseeing the logistics of the project. In the end the class raises two thousand dollars and donates the books during a celebration at the Kennedy Elementary School called the Gift of Words.

* * *

As we climb the stairs to Kennedy, Mary grabs Lori and squeezes her. "I'm so nervous. I can't believe this is happening." Mr. Quinn, standing off to the side, says, "Let's enjoy this, folks—you've earned it. This is *your* day. Your gift of words." Randy and Billy charge toward the multipurpose room but pause when they see the bustle of kids, teachers, and adults. Billy stops with the abruptness worthy of the Roadrunner—the epic cartoon character—"Holy shit, this is for real," he says with a low whistle.

Inside the room, the children were arranged in small circles of five or six students. At first the teenagers cluster in the back, but the teachers soon escort them to the kids. Each time a teenager joins a group, the children squirm with excitement. The superintendent and his cohort of officials stand against the far wall nodding em-

phatically at one another. Several newspaper reporters and pho-
tographers weave through the crowd. One teacher stands above a
group, hands on her hips, shaking her head at Ralph with a wry grin.
"I can't believe Ralph, Itchy Ralph, whom I had in second grade, not
only shaves but can read to these kids."

One poignant exchange that I witnessed involved Bobby, nick-
named Trailer, who is six feet tall and 240 pounds. He was one of the
few students who never came to Kennedy, and when he walks in the
room he stops and gawks. With his classmates bustling around the
room, Bobby sits down and fidgets, nervously slapping a rolled up
piece of paper against a meaty hand adorned with a thick cable gold
chain. One of the teachers comes by and grabs him by the arm. He
looks relieved somebody has noticed him, but he blanches when
they approach a circle of children. The kids look at him askance.
He's wearing a zippered up black windbreaker and he's shiny with
jewelry. His arms alone are thicker than any kid. Four kindergartners huddle up attentively, but one girl in a yellow dress can't find
her way into the circle and sits looking out at the crowd. It's an ironic
moment. Bobby, who often exasperates Mr. Quinn when he "checks
out" during class, says to her: "Hey, let's try and squeeze into the
circle. I think you'll like this book." She looks at him once and then
slides closer, giving him a big smile. Later, Bobby told me that her
smile was the best thing that happened to him the whole school year.

Feeling Good by Doing Good

Help thy brother's boat across, and lo, thine own has reached the shore.
—HINDU PROVERB

Toward the end of the ceremony I stood with Arnie, Billy,
Kobey, Trey, and Dave in the corner. The dignitaries had trickled
out, and the books had closed so that the ice cream could be opened.

The boys leaned against the wall and looked out with almost smug proprietorship. "You know," said Kobey in his understated way. "You know, it feels good to do good." There's a thoughtful pause before Trey teases him. "Dude, talking deep like Quinn." Over the months, Kobey's observation stayed with me. As I have tried to grasp the meaning inherent to the event, I have always come back to this comment as the essential explanation for why the Kennedy experience affected the students so profoundly

The goodness Kobey describes brings to its bearer more than pleasure. In his book *The Conquest of Happiness,* philosopher Bertrand Russell contends that there are two forms of happiness. The first he calls animal happiness, a state characterized by pleasure and contentment. The second type Russell calls spiritual happiness, which is a feeling of well-being that comes from an intellectual and emotional achievement.[1] Russell's notion of spiritual happiness resembles a state of well-being described by Aristotle called *eudaemonia.*[2] Aristotle asserts that we achieve deep satisfaction and happiness when we conduct our life with "actions in conformity with virtue."[3] In *The Call of Service*, Robert Coles offers a similar observation when he talks about the experience of a student volunteer he interviewed. "Over the years I have heard his sentiments echoed many times—the enthusiasm and pleasure, the exhilaration that accompany action taken, and the consequences of such action: deeds done, people very much touched."[4]

Coles and Aristotle would recognize Jen's response. "I like this experience because I walked away feeling as though I made a contribution and that feels right."

Connecting with the Young

Almost every student who participated in the Kennedy program noted the special feelings that emerged when they connected with a young student. They talked about feeling "connected to the kids" or "developing an ongoing relationship over time."

Often these alliances lasted for months and left the teens feeling that their influence contributed to the kindergartners' development. Mary's reflection illustrates this point: "One time, earlier in the year, I was sitting in the sandbox with several girls. They were crowding around me. Then I looked over and saw an adorable boy sitting by himself playing with some toys. He looked sad and lonely, so I approached him with a smile. I talked to him for a while and got him to come out of his shell. He opened up to me, and it seemed that although he was shy, I was able to connect with him and invite him to join us."

The relationship between Mary and this boy continued for several months. This experience reinforced her career goals. "I think I can connect to people like that boy. It confirms that I want to follow this dream to become a counselor or psychologist and help people like that boy."

Some volunteers experienced a connection to more than the children. Trey, for example, said that he felt "plugged into the community because I was working toward teaching reading, and that's something that's important to parents, teachers, employers. It's important to everybody." Andre explained that the project enabled him to connect to the community beyond his family. "My family really just stays together by ourselves. We're really close, but we don't interact with many other people, but I always wanted to help, or serve some other people. I think what made this really neat for me was that it allowed me to get beyond the little circle that I live in all the time." Mr. Quinn believed that students could make these connections because the program "sewed together disparate things. It connected many points: gender, age, community, skills, and schools. Being at the intersection of multiple points allows one to make sense of how things work, and that's meaningful for students."

Leaving a Legacy

Philosopher Robert Nozick contends that we desire to have an effect on the world. "When it's toward the good," he says, "it's wonderful."[5] The volunteers felt that their work meant something to the community and to the children. They believed that they influenced those children and that their influence would ripple outward. Lilia told me with earnest intensity, "Kids today are in real danger, and they don't listen to adults all the time. You know, when a teacher says something to you, kids just roll their eyes, but when we go over and we're adults, but not adults, they seem to listen to us, and because of that we had the opportunity to tell them stuff like reading is important and being nice to each other is important. One of the teachers thanked me for giving such a good message to her students. She said, 'They listen to you more than they would listen to me or their parents.' That made me appreciate how important our job was and it made me feel really proud." During a meeting with the grant director of the program, Trey described a similar perspective: "It's really great to know that people will listen to you. They're listening to us. They're listening! People don't have to listen, these kids don't need to listen to us, but they do. Since they're listening, you believe you're actually helping out kids by giving them good messages and being a good role model. Helping people and making a difference in the future. That's cool."

Lilia and Trey describe two facets of the volunteers' response to the program. First, they believe that they are having a positive and enduring effect on the kindergartners. Second, students relished being listened to, by the children as well as the adults, unlike in typical interactions at school. Vincent said, "People don't listen to us at school. Teachers talk at us or down to us." Mia also makes this point when she compares her job at Bloomingdales with her "job" as a student. "School's a jail for the most part, and we just clang our tin cups against the bars and nobody listens, nobody hears, or cares to hear what we have to say. I mean that's why I love work. I speak to people and they listen. They ask me questions and they want to hear my answers. Here nobody listens to me, or anybody else. It sucks."

Conversely, the kindergartners listened. "Their eyes followed me all the time," said Billy. Mary talked about how gratifying it was to have all the kids listening to her read. "I mean they were all ears. That felt so good." And Trey said, "The look on their faces when we began reading to them gave me a feeling unparalleled to anything else. . . . I could tell the joy that we brought to them, and it's something I hope others get to experience."

One testimonial stands out from a student who told me that he could barely make it through a school day because he became so frustrated just sitting and being talked at. He said, "When you first enter the classroom, all the children's faces light up with excitement and anticipation. Then they willingly follow you into the library and scamper to find their favorite book for you to read. Then they all huddle around me in anticipation of a great story. As the story progresses, they become more involved and start hanging all over you and climbing on top of you. Then when you leave, they seem so sad. But still there's excitement because next week you'll be back again to share with them the gift of words."

The high school students felt good to be role models for the kindergartners, and they also identified the specific role they had teaching kids about the power of reading. The irony didn't escape Mr. Quinn. "Some of my most reluctant readers, some of my kids who I don't think have finished a book in years are heading down to Kennedy to encourage reading." Room 36 was not filled with voracious, independent readers. A survey early in the year revealed that nearly three-quarters of the students disliked reading in school, and more than 60 percent said they never read books on their own. The resistance to reading troubled Mr. Quinn. "I'm frustrated with the cynicism toward reading this year. This year's group seems to just not read if they don't want to. You almost have to write the story yourself the night before to make sure it's text they encounter and not the 'Cliff Notes' or a movie. I find it very disheartening."

Reading may not have been a passion in these students' lives, but passionately conveying the importance of reading to the children at Kennedy was. One of the teenage organizers said, "I only read when I'm pushed to read by school. I mean pushed. It's not something I like, I mean I wish I liked reading more, but I just don't. I get so bored. But when I sit with those kids, I think that I can get them excited about reading and then they won't have the same problems that I do now."

Randy, who once confided to me that he had never read a full book in high school, sat with a boy nestled against his shoulder and said: "I want you to remember that reading gives you power— it makes you strong. I hope you remember that from this book." Randy told me later, "As the adult, or role model, you have to try and teach kids to do better than I do."

Another compelling element of this project was that it tapped in to the teenagers' sense of their position in the world. The volunteers felt that as young adults they were especially able to understand the problems that the Kennedy kids might face in school and in society. Some expressed a desire to protect the children. As one student said, "We get to play *The Catcher in the Rye* at Kennedy." In Salinger's novel Holden Caulfield says, "Anyway, I keep picturing all these little kids playing some game in the big field of rye and all. Thousands of little kids, and nobody's around—nobody big, I mean—except me. And I'm standing on the edge of some crazy cliff. What I have to do, I have to catch everybody if they start to go over the cliff—I mean if they're running and they don't look where they're going I have to come out from somewhere and *catch* them."[6]

Trey explains that the program addresses broader concerns than just reading. "Kids in today's world need help. I mean, even though the Kennedy kids are mostly good kids living in a good neighborhood, they still need some help, and that's what we're doing for them. We're helping take care of them, you know, like that 'it takes a village' thing." And Loren describes her sense of obligation to the younger students. "What's important about our work at Kennedy is that we're helping other people, particularly younger people. Things are really complicated for children now, so we, as older children, need to find ways to help them out. I sort of don't look at it as a choice but a must. I try and do this with my sister. I look out for her and give her advice and make sure she's doing her work—but what makes Kennedy so important is that we're doing this for a whole grade full of kids."

Writing about the dynamics of caring, educator Nel Noddings explains that the act of caring for others is obviously advantageous for the recipient but the relationship can also benefit the caretaker.[7] Dave's experience is a good example of this phenomenon. One day Mr. Quinn and I overheard him telling a fellow student "how cool" it was to go to Kennedy. Mr. Quinn told me more. "Take Dave, for example, he obviously is a kid in turmoil. He started out this year angry, sullen, and often detached. The first month he sat in the corner and barely acknowledged that class was happening around him. But he's become one of the most active participants in this Kennedy event. I think it's helped him open up, and he's really taken a leadership role in securing the grant for the books."

And Tristan shared her experience of benefiting from caring for another. "I'm sort of a misfit. I just really don't fit in. I feel alone lots of time at school. I never feel like I belong, or get attention for the right reasons." She once described her life as an "undone puzzle." Tristan's participation in the project generated much different feelings. "Going to Kennedy makes me feel so good about myself. I remember the second time I went to Kennedy, and I was standing around sort of uncomfortable waiting to be assigned to a group, and a big group of little girls all ran up yelling, 'We wanna be with you.' I loved that feeling because I remember when I was that age I looked up to people bigger and older than I was. At that moment, I realized that I finally had become that bigger, older person who was making a positive impact on these little girls." She recalled an experience that took place during the book donation ceremony:

> I remember I was sitting on the floor with my group, and this little girl kept staring at my shoes. It was cute because she would take her little hands and try to measure my platform heels. But the one thing that stuck in my mind was when I was standing in line with the kids waiting for ice cream, and it was noisy and chaotic, and all of a sudden I felt this little hand slip into mine. I looked down and it was the little girl who had been measuring my shoe. She gave me this smile, and I felt so good. I felt like I accomplished something and that somebody actually looked up to me for protection and safety and comfort. Every time I went to Kennedy and picked up a book I felt this feeling that I was doing something little that would affect these kids for the rest of their life. It was a great feeling! I would get goosebumps just thinking that I wasn't doing something for myself, but for someone else. I want to do other things like this.

The Kennedy program clearly had enduring and positive effects on the children and adolescents alike.

An Orienting Experience

Volunteering with the youngsters may have helped the older students clarify their sense of self. "If I had to pick one word that describes how I've been feeling this year," says Mary, "it would be confused. Yeah, that's it—confused." Adolescence is a developmental stage characterized by the formation of one's self-concept and values.[8] A teenager's sense of self is continually reevaluated, and experiences undergone can be formative and influential.[9]

This was illustrated for me in the middle of the ceremony, when I saw Lilia standing against the wall. She was holding an Elmo book and looking pensively at the kids. She told me, "This is so cool. It really is. I mean, this is something that's really helpful and good for lots of people. I mean, look at those kids with John. They're so interested and happy. I mean, when we started this I thought it was an O.K. idea, but now that it's happening I realize how important it is to devote time and energy to making these things happen." A few minutes later, I came across Trey, who was writing in his journal. I asked him if he would share what he wrote, and he did. "There's joy in every child in the room. Joy in the little kids, but joy in the big kids as well. What sums it up for me came when I passed out the books. One of the boys, a small Mexican child, hadn't said anything, but when I gave him the book his eyes lit up, and he began to flip through the pages. Learning is about relationships. I created that joy. That's what it is for me as a student, and now to see it as the 'teacher' really paints it clearer."

These reflections suggest that at least in this moment the experience helped Lilia and Trey clarify their vision of who they wanted to be. And another student said, "It made me realize how important I can be in the community. As this little girl sat on my lap, I had this sudden thought that I should do something like this more often." Students learned something about themselves and their ability to make an impact in the world: they described a more robust sense of being able to make things happen.

The belief in our ability to influence events that affect our lives is often described as self-efficacy. These beliefs determine how we feel, think, and behave. People with strong self-efficacy pursue challenging opportunities and persist in their efforts. Psychologist Albert Bandura identifies *enacted mastery*, which occurs from the successful execution of an activity, as the most important source of self-efficacy.[10] I noticed that those students on the grant writing team experienced a sense of enacted mastery. This group successfully raised the funds and organized the ceremony. Lilia, for example, became involved with student government the next year, and when I asked her why, she said, "The Kennedy experience made me feel really confident in my ability to organize things. I remember thinking at first that there's no way we could ever get a company to give us money. But they did. They gave us money after we convinced them of how important our plan was." She also said that she was planning other grant writing projects this year as part of her government platform.

Arnie had a similar response, "What I've really thought about since last year is that we came up with the idea and followed it through. I mean it was just a small idea, but it was like one stone rolling and knocking into other stones until it becomes an avalanche. . . . It makes you feel like you can accomplish more. Like, I've thought about wanting to be a famous actor. It is kind of like, jeez, that is such a long shot, but then I think about what happened with Kennedy, and I start to think differently. For example, I said, just get into drama and take this little step and then this little step. It kinda of pulls your goals a little bit closer to you."

A powerful mastery experience can also produce what Bandura calls a transformational restructuring of efficacy beliefs.[11] These moments of triumph encourage an individual's belief that he or she can exercise control over his or her own life. Several students extended the lessons gleaned from the Kennedy experience to other domains of their lives. For example, Arnie said that he was wavering about whether he could tackle summer school. A week after the project ended, he committed. "I mean if I could organize the 'Gift of Words,' than I could stick out summer school." Trey said that he was determined to re-create the experience during his senior year, "We started the next year out with just a regular English class and no Kennedy experience, but I really missed it. What we did last year was really important to those kids. I think we made a difference in their lives and it's something I wanted to continue to do. So I went with Jim to speak to my teacher, and we told her about last year, and she said that we could organize something if we wanted to. Well, we're going back every week to read at Kennedy."

These students not only exalted in the moment but carried the experience into their futures.

Cultivating Virtuous Activity in the Classroom

Our moral measure for estimating any existing arrangement or any proposed reform is . . . does it liberate or suppress, ossify or render flexible, divide or unify interest?

—JOHN DEWEY, *Human Nature and Conduct*

After the Gift of Words celebration, I joined Mr. Quinn in his room for lunch. His exhausted glow reminded me of interviews with triumphant athletes in the locker room. "You know, Sam, you know, I can't believe this came off so well," said Mr. Quinn. "I mean, who could ever have imagined that it would have turned into such an event. All I want to do is soak this in." He looks at his watch and winces, "But I've got to teach another class in five minutes."

The project did gain momentum over time. As Mr. Quinn said, "I certainly didn't have this extravaganza in mind when I set this up, but it really took on a life through the year." I suggest that three factors were critical to the project's growth and success. First, Mr. Quinn prevailed over the institutional constraints that often deter teachers from integrating nontraditional experiences in their curriculum. Second, Mr. Quinn's participation in the project is peripheral but pivotal. Last, being a volunteer at Kennedy became a mark of high status among the students; I consider how this reputation became a powerful engine.

Eluding the Constraints of the Institution

Many who have written about education describe the role of the school as a social institution designed to constrain and track students.[12] This research makes overt the practices and resources directed toward limiting freedom within schools. The most sharply critical theorists compare schools to penitentiaries.[13]

At Stanton High maintaining order and discipline is important. Its wide hallways are designed to accommodate the flow of students and enable a quick scan for whoever is out of place. Students need passes (as did I) to be in the hallway. Stanton prides itself on the decorum of its campus.

The year of my research the administration handed down controversial new rules cordoning off the parking lot during school hours. The policy infuriated many students. Mia said, "They treat us like we're fucking prisoners. I keep my books in my car. What the hell, do they think I'm going to go smoke a bong between Chemistry and English? It's like we have no freedom and no trust."

As at most comprehensive public schools, controlling student movement is a priority at Stanton. During lunch school service officers, administrators, and occasionally the police patrol the campus perimeter. Ostensibly these patrols prevent students from going off campus, but they also isolate the community from the school. Several students in Mr. Quinn's class were school service officers. When I asked Arthur what his duties were, he said, "Keep the freshmen in line." Teaching students to maintain and appreciate order in the school has its value; however, an initiative like the Kennedy project requires flexibility and tolerance for it to work. The differing ideologies are in conflict.

The design of the Kennedy program allowed five students to leave the campus once a week and walk unsupervised one-quarter mile to the elementary school. This sounds uncomplicated, but it's not at most public schools. At Stanton students must ask permission and carry a pass to go to the bathroom. And the liability issues that are associated with releasing students from campus are no small obstacle.

In addition to the institutional constraints that deter off-site educational experiences, teachers are often reluctant to interrupt their routines. If five or six students miss class each week, extra time is needed to make up their lessons. Mr. Quinn, for one, said: "I was willing to do this because I'm willing to give students the opportunity to have a different experience. I think being in class is important, but it's not sacred. Other teachers couldn't handle students missing their class."

In spite of the constraints Mr. Quinn decided to integrate the community service project into the curriculum. In his introductory letter to the students he wrote, "One last thing to mention. I have discussed with Mrs. Smith, the community service director here at S.H.S., the idea of linking our classes up with Kennedy Elementary. My hope is that we might be able to adopt an elementary school class, which we might, on occasion, visit and work with, perhaps reading them stories in cozy little groups. I've done it before, and it is worth the effort for all the good it does you. Think about it."

The letter suggests some of the ways that Mr. Quinn overcomes the institutional constraints. First, Mr. Quinn has help orchestrating this project, and teachers rarely have this kind of support. "I know this would have been impossible without Mrs. Smith," said Mr. Quinn. "I couldn't have managed the slew of details that come with doing community service."

Second, Mr. Quinn is willing for students to miss class because something good might develop. Yet this prospect is not enough for most teachers strained by increasing workloads.

Finally, Mr. Quinn recognized the value in an optional program with no explicit bearing on a student's evaluation. He writes, "Think about it" and this was his attitude throughout. He never coerced participation or required a commitment. The freedom and trust he granted the students contributed to the program's momentum.

Shadow Pedagogy

A powerful attribute of Mr. Quinn's teaching is a mode of involvement that I call shadow pedagogy. As Randy said, "Mr. Quinn was part of this, but he also wasn't part of it. He let us do this, but he helped us as well." Mr. Quinn quietly supported the grant writing team because he believed that the experience would have the most impact on students if they became the primary engineers. He told me, "I want to be the pipes that carry the water. I want to create the structure and the opportunity so this event comes off, but I want it to be run by the students on their own."

And later, reflecting on his role in the experience, he said, "I was transparent technology. I was the operating system in the background. The operating system is this infinitely complex backdrop that indiscernibly mediates everything that occurs. That's the role I strive to enact in many things in my class."

His commitment to shadow pedagogy manifested itself in many ways. He allowed the grant group to meet outside the classroom and rarely visited the group. When he did, he would ask: "Is there anything I can do?" It struck me as a powerful indication that he was willing to defer to the students. And during class he would ask, "Before I ask for volunteers for next week, how's it going over there?" After the report he'd say: "You guys are doing such a terrific job. I wish I could go one day and watch what you're doing." He deliberately cast the students as the experts to give them autonomy and a sense of proprietorship.

Teaching about Nobility

When some students met with one foundation, an administrator asked them to describe the program. Arnie said, "Essentially," he said, "we read books to the kindergartners." Trey added, "I guess it's not that we just go to Kennedy and read to kindergartners. But we do a lot of other things as well by being there. Like Mr. Quinn said about the book his son got from an older reader. Mr. Quinn's son cherished the book because he got it from an older role model, and that made him more excited about reading and probably helped him in other ways too." Mr. Quinn encouraged students to see that their work at Kennedy was a contribution to the community, an act of caring, and an intervention in the lives of young people.

As the year progressed, I came to appreciate Mr. Quinn's moral artistry.[14] He helped students see themselves as agents of virtue with the capacity to do important work. I recorded one example in my notes:

> Today Mr. Quinn read a brochure to the class about a new alternative program opening up at the local community college. The program is designed for disenfranchised high school students. Mr. Quinn said it was for "bright, creative, and disaffected students." After he finished reading, a flurry of questions followed about sports and extracurricular activities. Mr. Quinn asked, "Who would find this an intriguing possibility?" A thicket of fifteen hands shot up at the invitation. I can't help but notice the irony that even in this fine class, it takes an invitation to escape traditional school to get fifteen hands into the air. Randy called out, "It sounds less prisonlike than Stanton." Mr. Quinn said, "It's true. It offers more freedom and perhaps more dignity than the traditional institute of school. I have to tell you that it's immensely frustrating for me to look out at this class of thoughtful people. We're all so constrained by the institution of high school. . . . Yet, despite the constraints, you've found ways to be important in the lives of those children as mentors, guides, and role models. You're finding ways to make a difference.

Mr. Quinn helped the volunteers see the virtue in their efforts, and he gave them the language to understand why. But "cool" became the adjective of choice for the students when they talked about it. In fact, my interview transcripts offer countless instances where the word was used to describe the experience. Students even shared their enthusiasm for the program with their peers. One student said, "I told my friends that our class bought books for them [kindergartners] with money that was donated to us, and they said, 'Wow, cool.' " And from another, "I told a few of my friends about the Kennedy project and what it was like to read to them, and their immediate response was concern about how they could get involved with such a cool thing."

How did reading to kindergartners become cool? I think the experience tapped into the students' natural inclinations. The volunteers felt important, competent, and useful, and they liked being role models. According to Lisa, "I would walk in, and the kids would jump up to see me, and I would feel like a celebrity."

A second factor that contributed to how the program was perceived is related to social dynamics. Because high status students were involved, the project was seen by others as having some special cachet. I overheard a discussion between Trey, a popular kid, and Edgar, a more introverted student, during a class when Mr. Quinn asked who would volunteer that week.

TREY: Edgar, you been to Kennedy?
EDGAR: No.
TREY: You should go. Definitely, it's, like, really cool.
EDGAR: Nah, it's O.K.
TREY: I'm serious, I usually go with Sandra and Mike, and we have a great time. Serious.

Edgar changed his mind and volunteered. He told me, "I guess I just wanted to try it. Besides, Trey said it was cool." Trey's remarks included tacit recommendations from Sandra, a cheerleader, and Vincent, an athlete.

The role of peer leaders in the success of the project was critical. Research shows that effective youth projects require that students with leadership potential contribute positively.[15] The grant writing team was a high status group with significant social influence. Theo said, "Everybody likes Billy, Arnie, Mike, Lilia, and the rest of the group. If they're doing it, it makes the rest of us want to participate as well." Volunteering because it was cool may not have been the most worthy motivation, but what is important is that it helped the Kennedy program become hugely successful. In the end, students learned that doing good for others could be good for them, too.

CHAPTER 7

Tangling with the Unspeakable
An Episode of Facing
Conflict in Conversation

"Adults treat our generation as if we were infected meat," wrote Sal in his journal. Arnie says he can't walk down the street in Stanton without a senior citizen crossing to the other side. Jenny wrote an essay about how American adults view teenagers as lazy, spoiled, and materialistic. Students resent the media's simplistic portrayal of teenagers. As Lilia said, "They think since we care about our clothes, care about music, and care about MTV that we're just bubbleheads, but what they don't do is listen to what we're saying. We care about important stuff. They call our music noise, but it's about important issues like freedom and race. We think about that stuff."

I found that Mr. Quinn's students yearned to think and talk about weighty issues. They pondered surprisingly complex questions: who am I, who do I belong to, what do I believe, where will I end up? Sometimes, of course, they were shallow and self-absorbed, but when an opportunity was provided to think about how to live and who to be, more often than not they seized it.

In this chapter I recount a conversation about an issue of race and identity that is at the forefront of many teenagers' lives but is rarely discussed in private or in the classroom. The conversation was significant because the students were clearly fired up by the opportunity to address an issue that involves them all.

Important Talk

> What is true is that we make choices, that we choose voices to hear and voices to silence.
>
> —BELL HOOKS

The days before vacation always test a teacher's patience. Mr. Quinn has to make an extra effort to get the class settled before he begins. "We have to turn to something deeply serious and important." He's gripping his copy of *Huck Finn*. "Listen, you know this as well as I do, but it's hard to get anything done at the end of the quarter and with the holidays around the corner. I've been run ragged and I feel my own energy lagging. You also have been working hard, but today is not yet a holiday. You need to help me by staying with me because I intend for us to think and talk through something of importance."

Teachers build up a reserve of good faith with students. Today, Mr. Quinn tapped into that reserve. He hauled this group in from the hallway; they've already cranked into vacation mode, yet Mr. Quinn isn't ready to concede. He told me that he hasn't been happy about the pacing of the *Huck Finn* unit because there have been so many interruptions in the curriculum.. He has had to make time—about a class and a half each week—for test preparation for the state competency exams. This has been a source of considerable frustration for Mr. Quinn; students resent the test preparation and Mr. Quinn has found it difficult to pace the class's progress through *Huck Finn*. With vacation looming, students had not finished the book, but Mr. Quinn recognized that a ten-day hiatus would mean that he would have to almost begin again. He says, "I'm at a loss. I feel as though it's an incursion into the integrity of the book to not finish, but I recognize the lunacy of trying to begin again. I'm just going to forge ahead with what's essential in the story."

So plowing ahead, he tells the class: "I've mentioned that this book is controversial. It arouses deep passion in many, which to me is what books are supposed to do. Books are supposed to be controversial and engage people emotionally. If they don't then we shouldn't read them. Let's turn to the paper that I gave you yesterday describing what we're going to do." He reads:

> This week a group of parents formally demanded that Mark Twain's book *The Adventures of Huckleberry Finn* be barred from the classroom at Stanton High School. This group is comprised of parents and community members of different races— among which are included both whites and blacks—who based their argument on several assertions: The book perpetuates outdated and unjust stereotypes of African-Americans through its depiction of Jim and the use of the word "nigger" upwards of two hundred times. There are other books which can be read and studied as well to understand the nature of that period of our history and which are written from a more balanced cultural-historical perspective. The book, due to many of the reasons listed above and the fact that some classes at Stanton High have no African-American students to lend their voices to the discussion, harms those who read it because of its racial bias, which thereby harms the society as a whole by allowing this story to be told in American public classrooms.

Mr. Quinn looks up. "So, what do you think? For tomorrow you'll have to write a one-page response to these parents, but today we need to come together and talk about this. What are your thoughts?" The class looks uncomfortable. Then Sal blurts out: "I've got something to say. This year when we were playing Riverside [a predominantly African-American community] you could hear kids talking to each other. They were 'nigga this' and 'nigga that.' How come if it's so bad that these kids would be using it so much? I don't know why the parents would protest if their kids are using the term.

Seriously, why, if it's such a, I don't know, disrespecting word, were all these kids using the term?"

Later Mr. Quinn told me that he was a little taken aback. "I figured we would get into these kinds of issues slowly and gradually, but Sal floored it. We were into volatile in a flash." You could see kids sit straight up in their chairs. Billy whips off his hood. Hands fly up, and Mr. Quinn says, "I think you're asking a great question. What do other people think?" Trey speaks next: "Sal's comment reminds me of the comedian Chris Rock. Have you seen him? He uses the word 'nigger' every two or three seconds. I remember watching him once with my mother and she was disgusted. I remember her saying, 'I can't believe that he just used that word. What is he thinking?' I know that it's a word that he can use, but I don't think it's a word that somebody white can ever use." Alan volunteers: "I know there's something about that word that really upsets black people. I can remember once being down at the park with Billy. You guys know Billy right, he's the black kid who I'm friends with? Anyway, we were playing basketball one day, and this other black guy says, 'Good move, nigger' to him after he scored a basket. A few minutes later some white guy on my team said 'Good move, nigger' to him after he scored a basket. He didn't mean bad or anything, but Billy went crazy on this kid. He didn't mean anything derogatory by the way he said it, but Billy just went crazy. It was like it was O.K. for another black kid to say that but not for a white kid." Sal spoke again. "That reminds me of that movie we saw, *Glory,* with Morgan Freeman and Denzel Washington. We saw it in history class. Denzel Washington plays the angry soldier, and he tells Morgan Freeman, who is the sergeant, 'Nigger, you the white man's dog.' Morgan Freeman flips out and slaps Denzel and says, 'Who you calling nigger? Look at you,' and then he starts saying all this other shit like, 'I'm fighting for freedom and you just laying around complaining.' I remember that scene. It's like when he called him nigger, that was the worst thing he could say, and he just slapped him."

Hands are up all over the classroom, and the air crackles with tension. Mr. Quinn surveys the room and his eyes fall on Petrie. Petrie is soft-spoken and on most days sits in the corner. Mr. Quinn occasionally called on him, but since I'd been there, Petrie had never volunteered to participate. When he speaks now, his voice is robust. "I've got something to say. This reminds of the time in the second grade that I got slapped by one of my best friends because of using the 'n-word'. Seriously. A good friend of mine was black, and we were joking around when he playingly called me a 'white honky,' and I joked back and called him the 'n-word.' He stopped laughing and got an angry look on his face, and he went to tell the lunch monitor on me, and I got into big trouble. I remember telling the teacher that he had called me a 'white honky,' but she didn't care. I think I learned about that word from this incident, and I guess that if we read this book, we need to have these kinds of conversations and not just read the book."

"You see, you see," says Trey excitedly. "This is why we should ban this book. Here we are, a bunch of mostly white kids telling stories about how we saw black kids flip out when they were confronted with hearing the word 'nigger.' I think I understand why some people want to ban the book. Don't you think you would be hurt if you were black and you were listening to us?"

Sal answers, "I see what you're saying, but it's not if you say the word 'nigger,' but how you say it and to who and when all that stuff." Trey fires back: "You see, when you say that, you're not respecting the fact that it's a word that means that if you're African-American, two hundred years ago you were barely human. You weren't a man, and to use that word, no matter what the person who hears it thinks, is a matter of disrespect."

Mr. Quinn seems to sense a need for a little levity, "I'm glad there are desks between you guys." The comment gets an edgy laugh. "You're both passionate and thoughtful, and I'm finding this fascinating, but I want to think about how white people use this word and, in particular, Huck." He asks what the students would say to the parents who wrote the letter. Ashley goes first, "I would tell them that this book opens up an opportunity for us to talk about racism. C'mon, think about it. Do you ever remember speaking about stuff like this? No. I don't. We get mostly wrapped up in our own problems and forget about others. There's racism in this country, worse than we think. We need to find ways to talk about this stuff so we know about the narrow, racist ways some people think."

At this point, Mr. Quinn lets the students control the dialogue. After a few minutes of listening, he says, "You're making me so proud. Your comments are so insightful, but let me try and give you some background. Does anybody know the etymology of 'nigger'? Do you know where the word comes from?" "I think it comes from Negro," says Julia. "You're right," says Mr. Quinn. "It's from the French *negre,* which means black. What's important is that it became used by whites to slur black slaves and talk about them as if they were less than human. Language gets shaped over time. It's not static, but it changes and people change it. I think the question you're struggling with right now is of critical importance to all of us: Who owns the right to use a word that has such power? Let me give you an example of what happens when somebody uses language without permission. Let's take a teen word. Give me a word that you folks use." Someone calls out, "Dope." "O.K., that's a good one. What happens if you run down to the office, and your science teacher bumps into you and says, 'Gee, Sal, that's a really dope shirt you're wearing.' How do you feel?" Sal responds: "I feel like that person is ridiculous, because nothing sounds worse than when somebody tries to use language that doesn't belong to them."

Chris chimes in, "It reminds me of my coach who is always using our language. He tries to be cool, but it always sounds lame coming from him. It's awkward and even a little sleazy." Mr. Quinn nods. "I think we're getting somewhere here. It seems that what we're saying is that how we use language matters. From the parents protesting *Huck Finn* to Sal's experience during the football game to Petrie's poignant story to Chris's comment about the sleazy coach— language matters. My question to all of you is: What matters about language?"

Several hands shoot up, but Mr. Quinn encourages the kids to slow down and think. In the early 1970s educator Mary Budd Rowe championed the idea of providing uninterrupted time for students to reflect on and process a complex cognitive task.[1] She found that doing so allowed students to think through their own ideas and develop more fleshed out concepts. Mr. Quinn gave the class these moments by controlling the pace of a dialogue, sometimes in such subtle ways as, in this particular moment, a hand gesture.

After a pause, Mr. Quinn again asks, "How does language matter?" Hands fly up, but Mr. Quinn turns to Sal and says, "Since you started us off, I'm interested in what you have to say." Sal doesn't hesitate. "Language is dangerous. I mean, after that football game, I asked Ken, who's African-American, about why they were saying 'nigger this' and 'nigger that.' And he said, 'It's not just the word, but it's how you say the word. It depends on who says something, how they say something, when they say something, and what the look on their face is when they say it.' "

The discussion continued in this spirit. As the buzzer rang at the end of class, Mr. Quinn said, "I'm in awe of you folks. There's no way for a teacher to write a lesson plan that would evoke the quality of conversation that just transpired in this classroom. A conversation like this can't happen without your courage to be real, without your commitment to what's important. Thank you."

Thinking about Taboos

Unscrew the locks from the doors!
Unscrew the doors themselves from their jambs!

—WALT WHITMAN, *Song of Myself*

Weeks later I asked Petrie what he thought about this class, and he said, after a pause, "That class was really important to me. We need to learn to be open. We need to learn to share our feelings and have deep discussions about scary things. I think about this but I never talk about it with anyone. That's a word you can't say even to your friends. If you can't have such discussions then you should not read the book. Language is dangerous, but you can't learn about danger unless you confront it."

His response explains why the students had such strong reactions to that day's class: it was an open discussion about a sensitive and complicated subject. Months later Sal told me: "I think about racism all the time. It's in the videos I watch. It's in the music. It's in the magazines I read. It's just not talked about in the classes I take. I mean we talk about the history of prejudice, but we don't ever talk about how we should think about it now. It's an in-your-face topic for kids today."

In a critical ethnography of an urban school, Michelle Fine describes a culture of silence that pervades today's schools. She writes, "Silencing signifies a terror of words, a fear of talk."[2] It stifles expression and controls what can be spoken. It precludes honest and open discourse around such hot social issues as race and inequity. Fine laments the paralyzing impact of a curriculum that discourages adolescents from examining the serious issues in their lives. This culture tempers a teenager's natural desire to make sense of the world. As Petrie says, "How can you teach *Huck Finn* without taking on how the 'n-word' is used in our lives?"

The following year, for example, Trey was frustrated with how

Hamlet was taught in his senior-year English class. He was disappointed by the lack of focus on issues that were central to both the text and adolescent life. He said, "I know passion, and I know ambition, but all that we're supposed to know is who said 'the slings and arrows.' "

In *Releasing the Imagination,* educator Maxine Greene entreats teachers to make "an intensified effort to break through frames of custom and to touch the consciousness of those we teach. . . . Surely education today must be conceived as a mode of opening the world to critical judgments by the young and to their imaginative projections and, in time, to their transformative actions."[3] Greene envisions the ideal school as one where students learn to practice the intelligent critique of the status quo. She entreats teachers to create opportunities for students to question the state of our world. Her hope is to inspire critical thinking and deliberate action.

Reading the students' reflections, I got the sense that they were grateful to Mr. Quinn for allowing the discussion to take place. Trey said, "What I loved about that conversation was that we took on something controversial. We all have questions and opinions about this stuff, and we were trying to figure it out by talking about our experiences and asking questions. Then we focused on the way that language works in our society and how it has power and how certain people control it. We need to be thinking about that all the time."

Julia wrote: "I am mixed and I don't know what to call myself sometimes, and I'm always uncomfortable when other people name me or call me something. Having this conversation helped me understand why I'm so sensitive about this. I thought about it the other day when I had to check off my ethnicity on the SAT card. It asked what I was. I wanted to write, 'What am I? No box can ever tell you.' "

In his essay "On the Habit of Informed Skepticism," Ted Sizer invites us to think about what a wise society would be. He tells us that it would be full of young people whose zeal for asking who, what, why, and what if had not been crushed. "An interest in questions comes at birth. The 'why' questions abound, as many an exasperated parent will testify. That curiosity must be seized, with all the nuisance it causes. It must not be crushed, however disrupting it may be."[4] The teenagers in Mr. Quinn's room still harbored many 'why' questions; however, they were not questions about tame subjects. They wanted to know, for example, why the adults in Stanton were lobbying for a teenage curfew and why they wanted to banish *Huck Finn*.

Cultivating a Hospitable Space for Charged Conversation

Educational philosopher Jim Garrison writes that the teachable moment "all too often slips away before we can seize it. The teachable moment comes so suddenly and departs so swiftly that many of us assume it is simply a gift of good fortune."[5]

The conversation about race and language in Mr. Quinn's class was not a random event. It was made possible by a classroom environment that had been cultivated over time to hospitably receive such a charged discussion. Educator Parker J. Palmer has written about the kind of environment that encourages real conversation. "In the community of truth, as in real life, there are no pristine objects of knowledge and no ultimate authorities. In the community of truth, as in real life, truth does not reside primarily in propositions, and education is more than delivering propositions about objects to passive auditors. In the community of truth, knowing and teaching and learning look less like General Motors and more like a town meeting, less like a bureaucracy and more like bedlam."[6] I believe that Mr. Quinn's classroom represents this kind of environment and makes possible conversations that matter.

I once asked Mr. Quinn to summarize his teaching philosophy. "All of what I do, plan, and work for is to create a context for conversation," he said. "I think effective education is a conversation." He makes certain that his class understands this belief. At the beginning of the *Huck Finn* unit, for example, he told the students, "I'm reading it along with you. As I read, I make sense of the book, but the real learning for me and, I believe, for you occurs when we sit down and make meaning together. That's what learning is about. That's when learning happens."

Mr. Quinn knows that not just any discussion is effective for learning, but what he promotes is subject-centered discussion. In *A Passion for Excellence,* the organizational theorist Tom Peters and Nancy Austin identifies what he calls "bone-deep" vision as being essential to forging a successful culture. "Attention, symbols, drama. The nuts and bolts of leadership. More is called for than technique. You have to know what you're doing, to be able to state it clearly and concisely—and you have to care about it passionately. That all adds up to vision, the concise statement/picture of where the company and its people are heading, and why they should be proud of it."[7] Similarly, Howard Gardner, in his book *Leading Minds,* writes that a leader must convey an explicit statement of what is true, beautiful, and good, and in addition, must be able to tell a story about that message.[8] Mr. Quinn does this well—exceedingly well.

For Mr. Quinn, what is true and good is the ideal classroom, and he conveys to his students his vision of it. It is a place energized by conversation through both explicit statements and illustrative stories. He often told stories about the power of conversation in his own life. For example, he told students about letters he and his wife wrote to each other before they were married, while one was in Africa and the other was in Asia. He emphasized the role of conversation in learning to know a person. He shares stories of conversations with his friends, his sons, and his colleagues. He even told students about how his conversations with me had affected him. All these stories illustrate the same point—that conversations matter.

Hosting Conversation in the Classroom

During the heated and captivating exchange between Sal and Trey, the classroom felt charged. These two hulking young men, hats turned backward, fingers pointed at each other, were engaged in a back and forth battle that resembled a cross between hearty debate and talk show warfare. As I watched from my corner perch, I was transfixed by both the raw and vociferous energy being thrown off by the students and by my curiosity as an educator as to what Mr. Quinn would do next. Knowing what to do in a situation where there is robust intensity on the part of students around a controversial issue is a particularly thorny pedagogical dilemma.

In my fieldnotes, I called this the Daedalus-Icharus Moment. By taking the courageous leap to introduce this searing hot topic into the classroom, Mr. Quinn has given the classroom the power of flight. Now, Mr. Quinn, like Daedalus, watched as his students flew, perhaps, too close to the sun. Would this discussion become unglued? Would the fierce emotion being generated silence other students? How would other students find ways to become part of the discourse? And what should Mr. Quinn do? Can he intervene without shutting down the conversation? Do you let students charge ahead and risk this becoming an argument based on personal experience that loses all overt connection to *Huck Finn* and subject matter objectives?

As a teacher it is sometimes easy to read the intense energy of a discussion like this as the proxy for learning or constructive discourse around a controversial issue. When students are craned forward in their seats with their hands waving like a hillside of windmills, I cannot help but feel that their passion and attentiveness is better than docility; however, there have been so many occasions when I walked out of class feeling as if I had not capitalized on this surge of interest by channeling it more productively.

As Mr. Quinn told me earlier in the year, "Sometimes when they get going it is hard not be just a spectator." As I watched Mr. Quinn in this episode, he made some critical and intellectually responsible interventions and decisions that I believe deepened the discourse without stifling student voice.

First, as I watched Sal and Trey eye each other from across the room, I couldn't help but notice that, unlike every other classroom in this wing of Stanton High School, Mr. Quinn's students sat facing each other. In most classrooms, students talk to the back of other students' heads or direct their comments solely to the teacher. Mr. Quinn configured his room so that students could talk face-to-face, eye-to-eye.

Second, although students could have filled the whole period sharing personal positions and opinions on this subject, Mr. Quinn moderated and facilitated in ways that controlled the pace and flow of discussion. At times, he literally reins in the exuberance of the conversation by enforcing some moments of wait time; for example, shortly after he asked a question about how language matters, he asked, "What does Huck think when he looks across the raft floating down the Mississippi and looks deeply at Jim?" Again hands blast upward, but Mr. Quinn again intervened and said, "Before I hear from you, I'd like for you to jot down two or three sentences." Aside from slowing the pace of discussion, thereby providing opportunity for some students to coalesce their ideas through this 45-second writing assignment, I believe Mr. Quinn's intervention afforded students opportunity to engage in self-conversation. By turning them inward, Mr. Quinn gave them opportunity to register their perspective with themselves.

Third, Mr. Quinn managed to keep nudging the text back into the center of the discussion. "The hardest thing about a conversation like that," Mr. Quinn told me, "is to keep it from being solely self referential and judgmental." One way of understanding Mr. Quinn's questions in the discussion is through a model of questioning developed by educators Leila Christenbury and Pat Kelly. They developed a schema for engaging literature called the questioning circle.[9] It is made up of three intersecting circles: the matter, one's personal reality, and the external reality. Questions of matter focus predominantly on issues embedded in the text. Questions of personal reality deal with the individual's experiences, values, and ideas. Questions of external reality are about what is happening in the larger contexts of culture, history, and human nature. Christenbury and Kelly contend that questions that intersect all three domains are what they call dense questions, because they invite complex, flexible, and varied thinking.

While not adhering explicitly to Christenbury and Kelly's schema, Mr. Quinn's questions embodied each of the three domains, and his pivotal question could be understood as a dense question. For example, he asked questions of matter such as, "What are the variety of ways that Twain uses the word 'nigger' in the text?" This textual question sent students back into their books, and they spent several minutes flipping through pages hunting for examples. Early on in the lesson he keyed students into thinking about matters of personal reality when he asked, "Think of a time when you were the victim of a derogatory term. What emotions did this stir?" And when he asked, "Why is this such a taboo word in American culture?" he invited students to think about issues of external reality.

It is through these individual questions that he guided the conversation; however, his initial framing of the issue is what sets the stage for all that follows. The scenario that he shared involving the parents who protest the teaching of *Huck Finn* presents students with a "dense" situation that invites students to think about the themes flowing through the text, consider the social and political circumstances of their own community and the implications of using language, and to weigh this issue against their own beliefs, values, and ideals. The conversation that ensued honored the complexity of the issue. The text, the personal, and the external overlapped in ways that evoked a variety of compelling responses.

Lastly, and perhaps most importantly, this conversation succeeded in mattering to students because Mr. Quinn did not squelch it, silence it, censor it, or suffocate it by turning it into an opportunity to lecture students. He hosted the conversation that, as Judy wrote in her journal, stuck with students. "We need to learn to talk about these issues like race; if we don't then we're lost as a society. That's why everybody paid attention. We may not say it all the time, but we know this is what's important." It takes courage to invite taboo and charged topics into the classroom, but at least in this learning environment students were grateful for the chance to tangle with issues that live unspoken in their lives. As Mario said to me walking out class that day, "I wish we could have spent all day talking about this. We think about it all the time, but we don't really have a place to talk about it. At least not like this."

* * *

In *Teaching to Transgress*, bell hooks writes that throughout her years as a student and teacher, she has been most inspired by "those teachers who have had the courage to transgress those boundaries that would confine each pupil to a rote, assembly-line approach to learning."[10] Maxine Greene entreats us to teach in ways that invite "intensified realizations" and to "tap into imagination" so that we can see beyond what the imaginer has called normal or "common-sensible."[11] Teachers often chide the Greenes and hookses of the world for evoking "classrooms that are mere castles in the air." After a conversation with Mr. Quinn when I brought up the work of

Maxine Greene, he went home and read one of her essays. The next day he said, "I'm impressed, but how would she ever possibly 'release the imagination' in a class full of real-live teenagers?" I'm not sure what Maxine Greene would say, but I, for one, saw Mr. Quinn do just that the day the class tangled with the unspeakable.

CHAPTER 8

Caught!
Common Features in the Episodes

fter observing 124 classes and conducting hundreds of hours of interviews during my research, the moment that for me evokes the character of this project occurred one day in May. The classroom door has just closed behind the last student to leave room 36 on this day. As the door clicks shut, Mr. Quinn lifts his arms above his head like Rocky Balboa. He stands there, arms stretched to the heavens, an unopened yogurt in one hand and a handful of student papers in the other, and he lets out a primal whoop: "Yeah!"

His students had just finished a small-group discussion of words that describe the "personality of America." They wrote, they talked, and they argued. He had been at his best: asking questions, helping students reframe ideas, encouraging thinking "outside the box." He says to me now, "I feel utterly alive because they were utterly alive."

The state of being "utterly alive" is what Annie Dillard tells us to catch if we can. As Joseph Campbell told Bill Moyers, "People say that what we're all seeking is meaning for life. I don't think that's what we're really seeking. I think that what we are seeking is an experience of being alive, so that our life experiences on the physical plane will have resonance with our innermost being and reality, so that we actually feel the rapture of being alive. That's what it's finally all about."[1]

I want to talk now about those moments in the classroom when students feel the "rapture of being alive." They know when it happens. They feel it. They told me it is when their "insides leap" and when:

> You're reading something and it connects to what you're thinking and who you are; it's like a light bulb switches on and everything gets clear and focused. You feel alive.

> I was talking with my small group about the poem, and we got really involved. I was making my point, and people were listening, and when class is like that, it's great. Time flies and we're just talking with each other about things that feel important.

> I wrote a little bit of a poem today, and as I was writing, I felt completely awake to everybody and everything in the room. My first line was "I sit in the corner of the room / My eyes observing everything around me." I felt alert and keyed in to all that was happening.

These moments signify a taut, active commerce with the world. They represent an optimal state of consciousness, and students experience them as provocative, enchanting, memorable, and even enjoyable. These moments when students become roused to life and animated with feelings and ideas represent to me the highest attainable form of educational excellence; yet we seem to have little inclination to speak of teaching and learning in this way.

An Internet search for the terms "education" and "excellence" returns about 1,600,000 hits. The pursuit, attainment, and measurement of excellence are the rhetorical preoccupation and mantra not only of educators but of the larger society. As a notion excellence connotes superior performance or the exhibition of eminent qualities. In relation to education it implies high achievement and quality performance of both individuals and institutions. It's a keyword, tag word, and catch-all term that dominates the discourse. In the past few decades a spate of blue ribbon national reports have been written that can be characterized by their emphasis on the pursuit of excellence. Today, the same is true. We exhort excellence. We demand it. We count it. And we relentlessly attack schools and teachers for their failure to produce it in our children. Yet what is it? What is the nature of excellence in education? What forms of excellence does education aspire toward? Questions like these are complicated by what one believes is the purpose of education in our lives. A survey of today's educational landscape shows one notion of excellence predominant over all others—I'll call it fixed-end excellence.

Fixed-end excellence means that we set a standard, and if you reach the mark, you're excellent. It's a view that seeks to quantify the educational process in ways that allow us to track success and failure. This concept has the following properties: a) the standards of excellence and failure are determined prior to the activity; b) the standards are usually set by a central body that has little connection to the local setting; c) the standards are inflexible and those involved are expected to conform; and d) fixed-end conceptions of schooling allow for certainty: a school, or a student, is either excellent or not. When schools adopt this logic, excellence becomes something earned when explicit, quantifiable levels of performance are achieved.

From the *U.S. News and World Report* rankings of colleges to the annual rankings of regional schools in the local newspapers based on state and standardized test scores to the comparison of communities on the basis of S.A.T. scores, the discourse of excellence in American schools often focuses exclusively on calculations and averages based on fixed criteria. For example, when I was an administrator in California, the community where I worked had two high schools. One day a parent who was moving to the district scheduled a meeting with me to talk about which school her daughter should attend. She walked in with a handful of spread sheets and graphs comparing the two schools that a real estate agent had given her. The comparisons were based on test scores. She began by saying, "We're trying to decide which school is better, and based on all the information we have, this school is better." Sadly, her determination of quality was based on a statistically insignificant two-point differential in average S.A.T. scores.

In response, I suggested that she walk around the school and look and listen to the place at work. Look in classrooms, walk the hallways, speak to students, sit in on classes, come to our athletic events, attend our drama performances, stop by the office that arranges community service placements. Look, listen, and consider the way we live together and undergo our daily existence and interactions within this school. We diminish the enterprise of schooling when we make judgments about educational quality solely by narrow and fixed indicators. Achievement on academic litmus tests like the Advanced Placement and S.A.T. exams present one form of important evidence for us to make judgment about a school's performance, but when we discount the quality of the nitty-gritty, everyday interactions that are the essence of a school, we're as guilty of cooking the books as an Enron executive. Excellence must mean something more than mere academic achievement as measured by standardized tests. The triumphs or failures of schools involve dreams, hopes, relationships, and other abstractions that elude fixed-end calculations. No fixed-end system, for example, could measure the importance of moments of inspired learning. In fact, a fixed-end system would not even recognize their value.

The moments described in this book are occasions of exuberance, joy, power, and impact. They are memorable, and in their aftermath, students and teacher are left arms thrust heavenward in recognition and appreciation of their achievement.

Tuning In, Connecting, Brimming Over

Moments of inspired learning are difficult to capture, hard to define, almost impossible to replicate on command. But what we can do is talk about what makes them happen. What distinguishes an episode of inspired learning from a more prosaic classroom episode? In my analysis I identified a sequence of three interconnected experiences. First, students tuned in to the lesson with sustained focus. Second, once students were concentrating they forged a predominantly emotional connection with the material. This got students fired up. Third, once they were focused and passionate about the material, they were given the opportunity to express their thoughts.

I begin by sharing another episode drawn from Mr. Quinn's classroom. I focus on the experience of one young man to illuminate the three features of inspired learning.

Class begins with Mr. Quinn handing out a list of tasks the class is to complete by the end of the week along with their essays. The class seems both anxious and cranky. "O.K., you can do this," Mr. Quinn says, feeling their blues. "You're going to do a great job, and if you're feeling uneasy, you're probably confused, so come see me. I mean it."

He spins around once and claps his hands, loud enough that Lizza lets out a squeal of surprise. "Lizza, sorry for stopping your breathing, but it's time to shift gears. Let's go, go, go!" He points to a list he's written on the board: work, job, career, vocation, and profession. "All right, let's group up, really quick." Class dissolves into noise as desks turn toward each other. "O.K., let's devise a definition for each of these terms."

Mr. Quinn often breaks the class down into smaller groups so that the students can think through an idea with one another before returning to full-class conversation. When this happens, I typically pull up a chair and join any group. This time I sit next to Mario, a tall, handsome young man who had transferred back to Stanton to resume an academic program after he had attended a "vocational program" working in an office setting three days a week and taking classes the other two. A productive and interesting conversation ensues among the four students in the group as they attempt to differentiate the terms.

Mr. Quinn interrupts after a few minutes and says, "This is more fertile ground than I actually thought about when I devised this plan. Let's move back to our big-group formation and transition to what comes next. Before we talk through your categories of definition, which I found thoroughly interesting, I'd like you to listen to a poem that has always meant a great deal to me." Mr. Quinn reads Philip Levine's poem "What Work Is."

As I listen to Mr. Quinn read I watch Mario, whose reaction is pretty typical—students are often baffled by the poetry he brings in. Mr. Quinn senses the collective hesitancy and says, "O.K. folks, I'd like to direct your attention toward an important line in this poem for all of us to think about. Let's all look at line number two. I'll read it again, and then I want you to respond in writing to what you think Levine means. Here we go, and keep in mind what you talked about in your small group. 'For work. / You know what work is—if you're / old enough to read this you know what / work is, although you may not do it.' "[2] I'm sitting next to Mario, and as Mr. Quinn reads, he follows along with his index finger. His face morphs from furrowed to calm as he re-reads the line to himself. After a few seconds he begins to write:

"Working in the office last semester was work. Boring, mindless, boring work. Hauling sloppy dishes off a table is work. Knowing that my mom is out of the house before I rise is work. But do I know what work is—that is, real work? What is my real work, and when am I going to figure it out?" This poem, this subject, this class now means something to Mario. He began class typically diffuse and skeptical, but he's now focused and invested.

The class turns to a discussion of the terms on the board. Mario seems to me to be absorbed by what's unfolding: he raises his hand frequently, nods while others talk, and jots some notes down on the margin of the poem. When the class is over, I ask him what it was like for him today. He told me: "That poem made me think a lot about things that are happening to me. I'm trying to figure out what comes next and what I'm supposed to do. Work seems far away but it isn't. It was like that poem was getting me to think about questions that I need to think about, but I don't. That line about 'knowing what work is' makes me think about what my work will be. Will I be a guy who owns a restaurant? Will I be somebody who works with computers? Will I enjoy what I'm doing? Because so many of the people I met in that office hated, absolutely hated, freaking work."

This class had an impact on Mario. It woke him up, made him think, and provoked an emotional response.

Tuning In: The Contribution of Attention and Focus

The first characteristic of an inspired learning experience is focus. Focus suggests absorption and engagement in a particular activity. It means being attentive and interested so that energy and concentration converge. Maintaining our students' attention is a fundamental challenge of teaching. Consider how much of "teacher speak" is about capturing and holding the class's focus: "Pay attention," "Let's see your eyes up here," "Watch me," "What did I just say?" Teachers understand that what and how an individual learns depends on the quality of attention devoted to the task at hand. Teachers also understand that classrooms swirl with information and stimuli, and that competition for an adolescent's attention includes the magazine stuck under the book, the beeper that buzzed in the bag, as well as the complex social dynamics playing out in the classroom. A teacher vies for attention against some rather compelling distractions.

Attention is hard to measure and elusive to document; however, it is difficult to accomplish any educative outcome without marshalling the attention of students. If we aspire for classroom activities to be memorable and compelling, the important thing to maintain is a constant stream of focused concentration—total absorption in the activity. As William James writes, "Everyone knows what attention is. It is the taking of possession by the mind, in clear and vivid form, of one out of what seems several simultaneously possible objects of thought. Focalization, concentration, of consciousness are of its essence. It implies withdrawal from some things in order to deal effectively with others."[3]

Mario's experience mirrors the sequence James describes: When Mr. Quinn begins to read the poem, Mario's response is diffuse. His eyes and attention flit about the classroom. At one point he rolls his eyes at Jenna. He told me later that during the first reading, "his mind jumped all over the place." The moment that James would call "focalization" occurred when Mr. Quinn re-read the second line of the poem, "For work. / You know what work is—if you're / old enough to read this you know what / work is, although you may not do it." Mario's attention was caught. It is, however, what happens next that elevates this routine class encounter to something more intense.

Connected and Fired Up:
The Contribution of Feeling and Thinking

Securing a student's attention is only an avenue to something more substantial. What sets some classroom episodes apart from others is that the attention is accompanied by a significant emotional investment in the experience. These emotions then work in concert with our intelligence to produce a valued, memorable experience.

The role that emotions play in the life of the classroom has been profoundly neglected in educational research. Educational psychologist Robert Sylvester condemns educators for not focusing more on the role of emotions in learning:

> Our profession pays lip service to educating the whole student, but school activities tend to focus on the development of measurable, rational qualities. We measure students' spelling accuracy, not their emotional well-being. And when the budget gets tight, we cut the difficult-to-measure curricular areas, such as the arts, that tilt toward emotion.
>
> We know emotion is very important to the educative process because it drives attention, which drives learning and memory. We've never really understood emotion, however, and so don't know how to regulate it in school—beyond defining too much or too little of it as misbehavior and relegating most to fit it to the arts, P.E., recess, and the extracurricular program. Thus, we've never incorporated emotion comfortably into the curriculum and classroom.[4]

Emotions were palpably present in the moments of inspired learning that I identified; they were the fuel that made these spans of time glow. It is important that the presence of emotion is not seen as an indication of the absence of thought. Feeling and thinking worked in concert to fire up students in these moments. In his book *In Praise of the Cognitive Emotions,* Israel Scheffler discusses the reciprocal partnership of emotion and cognition. He writes, "Emotion without cognition is blind, and, as I shall hope particularly to show . . . cognition without emotion is vacuous."[5]

In Mario's response we saw the dynamic intermingling of thought and emotion that Scheffler describes. For example, his insight into his mother's relentless commitment to his well-being is not clinical and sanitized but is pulsing with intensity. During these classroom episodes I witnessed a full spectrum of zesty emotions: excitement, anxiety, anger, despair, and joy. I came to believe that the presence of emotions was an indication that students believed that the subject was something of value. Philosopher Martha Nussbaum, in her book *Upheavals of Thought: The Intelligence of Emotions,* expands this observation. Nussbaum's central thesis is that "emotions are appraisals or value judgments, which ascribe to things and persons outside the person's own control great importance for that person's own flourishing."[6] In other words, she argues that emotions involve judgments about what's important. We feel emotion when we recognize that an object of focus is relevant to our own well-being. In one of the surveys I conducted, a student reframed this point well: "School really matters when I believe that what's happening might actually mean something to me beyond just merely doing what I'm supposed to."

Nussbaum also tells us: "The object of the emotion is seen as important for some role it plays in the person's own life."[7] Emotions connect us to something; they are impulses directed at a specific object. The poem triggers some anxiety in Mario; he's focused on his future, and what lies ahead is scary.

In each of these special classroom episodes, students described feeling a connection between the subject under study and their own well-being. This becomes a "live encounter between the knower and the known."[8] In this potent encounter emotion and mind commingle, and the result is what Nussbaum calls a "geological upheaval of thought."[9] I observed two things happen when these encounters arise. First, students tune in. That is, they become focused on the subject matter. Second, when the mental spotlight is focused on a subject matter, this active engagement yields ideas, insights, and connections.

Brimming Over: Generative Thinking

The last feature common to the moments of inspired learning that I observed might be the most critical. When students tuned in and connected, they became dynamic, awake, and vital. They entered a generative state, brimming over with ideas, insights, and sensations. The antithesis of this fertile state is one of inertness, which Alfred North Whitehead, in his classic treatise *The Aims of Education,* warns us is the loathsome enemy of learning and education.[10] Inertness is passive; the mind drags along with lethargy and lassitude.

Comments from students are suggestive of this generative state. "Reading this gave me lots of new ideas"; "hearing those comments made me think differently"; "writing that journal opened up a new way of thinking things"; "I can't believe how many ideas zoomed through my head when I read that poem." In this state new and original ideas are produced. Philosopher Robert Nozick writes that generativity "itself is important, not simply the new and novel product, I conjecture, because the personal meaning of such creative activity is self-transformation."[11] In other words, the experience of producing new ideas or encountering fresh insights results in a variety of intense emotions.

During his encounter with the poem Mario was popping with ideas, sensations, and impressions. He generated ideas about his own future and his mother's work. An episode of generative thought contributes meaning and value to our lives, and it modifies our perception of the world. It changes the way we know our world.

Generative thought can also produce tangible expressions of original thought. Students might express themselves verbally to the class, write a poem or an essay, or create a project that describes how they understand themselves in the world. In a seminar at Duke University titled "The Search for Meaning," students are taught that we feel most alive and experience our life as better, richer, and more interesting when we feel creative. "Human beings are animals who eat, reproduce, live, and die. Yet unlike other animals we also appear to have both a great need and a great ability to create. We are *Homo fabricator,* people who make things. We are rarely content to leave the world as we have found it. . . . To carve a whist, to build a fence, plant a tree, make an apple pie, to paint the ceiling of the Sistine Chapel, to replace the valves on a 1952 Chevrolet—we are often most alive, most ourselves when we are engaged in some act of creativity. Creativity transforms us from a detached observer of life into a responsible participant."[12]

The students in Mr. Quinn's class were most alive, most engaged, most provoked when they were generating ideas, insights, and understandings of the world. These moments are what Joseph Campbell calls the "rapture of being alive," and they came about as a "live encounter" between the subjects and the students.

In my research these moments of inspired learning shared certain elements: when a teacher stirred the interest of a student so that the student tuned in and discovered an emotional attachment to the subject. When this connection occurred, students got fired up in ways that allowed them to brim over with the ideas that altered their view of themselves and the world. I now turn to thinking about what a teacher can do to cultivate these types of experiences.

CHAPTER 9

A Letter to a Colleague

Dear Adam:

We've been in touch ever since you sauntered into my classroom twelve years ago as a jolly, broad-shouldered fifteen-year-old. I can still remember you reading the haunting and beautiful biography you wrote about your grandfather's military service. I can remember our fishbowl exercise when you did a role play as William Golding and we interviewed you about the themes in *Lord of the Flies*. Perhaps the most meaningful tribute ever paid to me as a teacher was your letter that said you were becoming an English teacher because of the inspiration and experience you had during your sophomore year in my class. Over the years we've talked about the craft of teaching, and you've shared with me many extraordinary moments you've had with your own students.

Throughout this project I've thought of you often as the audience for this book. You represent to me the best our profession has to offer: a young, promising teacher who is brimming with passion and heart for your subject, your students, and the venture of education. Occasionally you've asked me about my research project, and when I told you, you respond like most teachers do when I explain that I've been searching to understand those compelling moments when we come together with our students. You nod knowingly, then ask what I can tell you so that you can create these moments more frequently. It's a worthy question, and I address it here in this letter to you.

It is important to say that this letter could easily be one that I write to myself. Perhaps the best definition of teaching I've ever read comes from William Ayers in his book *To Become a Teacher*. He wrote, "Since teaching is always a search for better teaching, I am still in a fundamental sense becoming a teacher. I am stretching, searching and reaching toward teaching."[1] I've probably taught twelve thousand classes in my career, and I'm still fundamentally stretching and searching for ways to serve my students better. The year that I joined Mr. Quinn's students was a year of the greatest professional development I've ever had. I spent those months talking with thirty-two teenagers and one exuberant teacher about learning and teaching. It was a gift. My hope is that I am giving something back now with this letter. I write it for you and for all teachers who want to better serve their students and themselves. Consider it a brief sketch of the ways that we can cultivate moments of inspired learning in the classroom and, in the process, continue "reaching toward teaching."

Cultivate Rapport with Your Students

I know you have a knack for this already. You've told me that knowing your students brings you great joy and reward. Continue to forge connections with them; it's the heart of the work. The more you know who they are, what they stand for, how their minds work, and what pressures shape them, the more you will be able to create opportunities for powerful and engrossing learning.

Many of the best teachers I've known seem deeply tuned in to what their students are experiencing. It's never been clear to me whether they possess a special knack for empathy or just the disposition and commitment to listen to what their students are saying about their lives. Listening to the students, I realized time and again that they think and feel about the world differently than adults do. Children's book writer Edith Nesbit said when she was a child she used to "pray fervently, tearfully, that when I should be grown up I might never forget what I thought, felt, and suffered as a child." We may not intend to forget, but we do. Even if we think we remember the vagaries of our own youth, we must recognize, as I know you do, that there is a diverse array of young people in our classrooms. We must learn about the sources of heterogeneity within our classrooms. Aside from respecting and honoring that difference, our job is to know their fears, aspirations, idiosyncrasies, and aptitudes. And just when you think you know them, remember Ted Sizer's advice, "There are no perfect tests one can administer to get a permanent fix on a child, no matter how educators struggle to create such devices and to believe in them. Current research on learning and adolescent development is full of speculation, of conflicting findings and incomplete results, and it gives no simple answer to the nature of learning or growing up. In sum, teachers (like parents) are very much on their own, drawing on a mixture of signals from research, from experience, and from common sense as the basis for their decisions."[2]

Mr. Quinn worked relentlessly, using various ways, to get to know and understand his students. His knowledge of his students and their relationships directly and indirectly contributed to the charged experiences I observed. I believe students engaged with the material more often in Mr. Quinn's class than in other classes because they knew he cared about them. As one girl told me, "I could be invisible, for all the notice that I get from most teachers. But I feel like Mr. Quinn really knows me and when somebody like Mr. Quinn knows me, I find myself doing more."

Mr. Quinn also used his knowledge of the teenagers' experiences to create bridges of meaning between the subject under study and the issues in students' lives. In chapter eight I highlighted one class when Mr. Quinn read Philip Levine's poem "What Work Is." A few days before this, the guidance counselor had come to speak with the class about career and college choices. The group was unusually somber as they listened to the counselor rattle off due dates and impending decision points. After she left, some students muttered that they hadn't thought about it yet and that they hadn't known where to begin. After class, several students talked about their anxiety around what they wanted to do after high school. Mr. Quinn's response to their apparent dislocation was to invite them to think with Levine about the distinctions among work, career, job, and vocation. Mr. Quinn listened, heard their disequilibrium, and then devised an encounter for them to awaken to an issue at the forefront of their lives.

Building good relationships also earned Mr. Quinn the trust to experiment with those unconventional approaches that more often led to intense experiences. Students would balk, but they never shut down. As one student said, on her way to the assignment in the outfield, "If this wasn't Mr. Quinn, there's no way I'd do something crazy like this."

Adam, I know that you, like Mr. Quinn, seek out students and work hard to engage with them. Here I would like to share with you some of his strategies for creating connections with the class. As he told me:

You do some of your best teaching when you're not in the classroom. Management guru Tom Peters champions a revolutionary approach for leaders and managers that he wryly calls the "technology of the obvious." By this he means management by walking around. If you walk around, listen, and ask questions you'll stay in touch with what is tangible, real, and visceral. Mr. Quinn knew something about his students, and they appreciated that he did. He went to their games, he admired their new cars, he stopped to chat in the hallway. As one student said, "What I like about Mr. Quinn is that he always makes sure to say hello to me in the hall. And when I come in to class, he looks at me and asks how things are going. Sometimes he asks me about the team and our next game. He's interested in me as a person."

Create opportunities, both structured and informal, to listen to your students. Mr. Quinn incessantly checked in with students. As they walked into the classroom, he would stand by the door asking, "How are things going?" or "What was the score of last night's game?" As he moved around the classroom during small-group work, he would see a CD-player on the desk and ask, "What are you listening to?" He soaked up opportunities to know them. It is significant that his classroom was open during lunch and after class. Kids came to hang out, use the computer, escape the muck and clatter of the lunchroom, or practice their breakdancing. Mr. Quinn's room was a place to go, and the informal interactions were often rich and caring.

He employed more formal mechanisms as well. One was that he frequently had students write for a minute about a particular question. The prompts he used were not elaborate. For example, "How do you plan on doing better this semester?" "What do you think of *Cannery Row*?" "What's going well on this project, and what do you need help with?" "What are your plans for vacation?" He also had students fill out questionnaires about themselves, write essays about their high school careers, and keep journals.

Devise assignments that advance your content goals while giving students an opportunity to explore their inner lives, the trajectory of their future, and their place in the world. Here's a sample of the many projects and questions that I observed Mr. Quinn present in this spirit:

- Where I Have Been, Am, Will Be: Senior Reflections on Life: Generate a portfolio of episodes that include such pivotal events as when you first crawled, walked, went to nursery school, elementary school, hit your first home run. List the accomplishments in life so far—no matter how small or large. List all the important conflicts, obstacles you have faced, and how you have or haven't solved them. Stephen Covey said, "Hey, it's your funeral, Mac." What do you want people to say about you at the end of your life?
- Antigone Essay: We define our self through our actions. We reveal our character in situations when we face dilemmas. Recall an incident in which you revealed something significant about yourself that taught you something—maybe even something that was not easy or pleasant to learn. In the course of your essay, please be sure to discuss what the actions of Antigone, Creon, and Ismene revealed about themselves.
- The Holden Project: This will give you an opportunity to explore a theme in *Catcher in the Rye* using words, images, and sound. Consider the opening line of the novel: "If you really want to know the truth . . ." Everyone *but* teenagers is always talking about what is important to teenagers, what you want, how you feel, why you act the way you do, why you dress the way you do. Pick one aspect of teenage life—fashion, relationships, parents, music, teenage stereotypes in the media— and do some work investigating your subject so you can learn more about it and teach us.

The benefit of these kinds of assignments are multifaceted; Mr. Quinn's questions resulted in an ever-open, always coursing pipeline of salient information about the students' lives that he used to advance the learning that unfolded in his classroom.

Recognize students publicly and privately for what makes them proud. Mr. Quinn made a point to figure out what made each kid special and acknowledge it. From Arnie's bodybuilding to Theo's budding baseball career to Linda's horseback riding to Trey's love of exotic cars to Jimmy's computer programming, Mr. Quinn found a way to know and recognize their special passions. And when teachers know students well, students believe they matter, and when that happens, they're more willing to be engaged.

I once read about a young writer who followed what he called a sacred tradition. On the first of every month, without fail, he read *The Adventures of Huckleberry Finn* for inspiration, instruction, and grounding. It struck me as a pilgrimage back to the heart of the matter. The journey from the front of the room as a teacher to the back of the room as a researcher hanging out with students was also a pilgrimage to the heart of the matter. If I could suggest one habit of practice that you should adopt, one sacred tradition to adhere to at least once every year, it would be to shadow teenagers through their classes, through the parking lot, and to their after-school jobs. See their world, hear their world, and feel their experience. We forget.

Compete Tenaciously for Their Attention

Recognize that these teenagers are unabashed and savvy consumers of many things. These kids carry credit cards, billfolds, cell phones, and pagers. They understand that the inalienable right of a consumer is the power to choose. They are experienced and intelligent consumers who know how to discriminate. They have come of age at a time when vast segments of the economy and the media vie relentlessly for their affection, interest, and, ultimately, their pocket books—which is estimated to collectively hold $155 billion in spending power annually.[3] Almost all the students in the class worked after-school jobs (27 out of 32) and many received other money from allowance. They were full-fledged shoppers, and I often sat in on elaborate conversations that described the merits and failings of new products from pagers to cars to clothes to music. From the hundreds of channels on cable to their budding financial autonomy, I was struck time and again by how accustomed they were to making choices about to whom and to where they allocate their attention.

A. Bartlett Giamatti, past president of Yale University and commissioner of major league baseball, said, "We can learn far more about the conditions, and values, of a society by contemplating how it chooses to play, to use its free time, to take its leisure, than by examining how it goes about its work."[4] The youth that I worked with in Mr. Quinn's class spent their free time engrossed with products that entertained and absorbed them. We need to recognize that these kids know how to have fun.

As Elissa Moses, a marketing executive who has written extensively about the disposition and desires of youth culture, observes, "Today's youth have an insatiable appetite for ubiquitous entertainment. Music goes with them. Games go with them." Their quest for constant entertainment is linked to what Moses describes as a quest for endless sensation, "Global teens have been brought up to experience and to expect sensory stimulation. This generation is constantly looking for new thrills that entertain. The preferred music is loud. The movies enjoyed feature fast action. The dances are rhythmic and frenetic. These teens are energy in motion. The craving for new sensations leads these teens to test their mettle and push to the extremes. They play out life to the max. Global teens have a very low threshold for boredom, and this is an essential finding for marketers: Do not bore this generation or it will abandon you."[5]

I was repeatedly struck by the students' consumer mentality toward school. If school didn't intrigue or excite them, they mentally abandoned the classroom. Simply put, they tuned out. They were a tough audience. One of my compelling memories of the class occurred when Mr. Quinn was trying to teach a series of lessons on the comma. He stood up there working hard to hold their attention. I saw Jessie slip her hand into her bag and pull out a J. Crew catalogue. Pick the analogy: she changed the channel, she tuned out, she left one store in the mall and went to another.

Maybe sometime in the future *wild technology* will bring us an "attention surveillance system" as presented in a book by Thomas H. Davenport and John C. Beck called *The Attention Economy*. They describe using attention technologies to monitor students' focus in a classroom: "A classroom might be outfitted with a panel of lights at the teacher's workstation, one light corresponding to each student's seat. If a student is paying attention, brain wave monitors note this, and the student's light is green. If the student's attention lags, the light goes red. When the teacher notes a red light, rather than rapping the student's knuckles with a ruler, he or she engages the student's attention by asking a question, focusing his or her voice in the student's direction, waving the arms wildly, or whatever."[6]

Mr. Quinn didn't have the technology to monitor brain waves, but he did what he could to catch and hold their interest.

Embrace your role as a performer.

You are on stage and your students are in many ways akin to a captive audience. They file in, sit down, and look up at you, waiting to be moved, entertained, changed, excited, intrigued, or bored. During my year of participation in Mr. Quinn's class, I felt like an audience member taking my seat for a performance. I'd look up at Mr. Quinn and wonder, where will today's episode go? His gift was not in performing a script but in understanding what engaged his audience.

Seymour Sarason, in his book *Teaching as Performative Art*, argues that teachers are actors who would be well served to use the traditions of stage performance to instruct and move an audience. He explains that an audience possesses "diverse expectations," but among them the most important is that the performer will "get them out of themselves," will transport them willingly and unreflectively to another world. When that audience is bored, unbelieving, and their thoughts, feelings, and fantasies are unrelated to performance, we say the performer has "lost" the audience.[7] Sarason argues that the artistry of performing teachers is in their ability to know what members of the audience need, think, feel, hope for, and understand. Having this knowledge combined with a sense of your own self as a theatrical agent allows you to modulate your teaching based on the extent to which you understand whether your students are stimulated, moved, energized, responsive, or detached.

Give your classroom character.

Mr. Quinn's classroom had texture, history, and character. He created a themed environment that actively aimed to convey symbolic meaning to its inhabitants. The room was rich with stimulating books, posters, photographs, projects, and piles of paper. It was a distinctive space filled with motifs and symbols of literacy. As one student said, "All it needs is a cappuccino machine and it could be Quinn's Coffee Shoppe for Writers and Poets."

It was also designed to be an enclave. The vitality of its decor starkly contrasted with the colorless hallway and the drab of the surrounding classrooms. Nobody could see in because of the collage of photos, articles, and other decorations covering the window. Likewise, Mr. Quinn rarely kept his door open. He created a distinct bounded and stimulating microculture in the room.

Tap into their senses.

That is, don't just talk and read but engage the senses. Mr. Quinn asked the class to experiment with different ways of perceiving. He played music during journal writing, brought them outside, asked them to close their eyes and visualize. He asked them to expand their notion of what constitutes a text by arranging encounters with film, music, audio books, photographs, artwork, spoken poetry, and sculpture.

Manipulate time, pacing, and rhythm, and plan novelty and surprise. There was something perpetually impending in Mr. Quinn's class. He was famous among the students for his extensive weekly calendars that he gave students every Monday that accounted day-by-day for the assignments, readings, and planned activities. Aside from the hard-charging pace of activity in the classroom, class just felt intense. The room seemed like a busy, industrious workshop.

In spite of the busy rhythm to the class, there were moments of designed serenity. Some moments of meaning-making require serenity to fashion the time, space, and solitude necessary. The class in the outfield, for example, relied on solitude to forge meaning from the plot of grass. Students were given private time for writing. Mr. Quinn held the calm times as sacred. He would play music, dim the lights, and ferociously protect the space from disruptions. I came to understand that busy and edgy came naturally to the classroom; serenity needed to be staged and orchestrated.

Acknowledge boring.
No matter how you package some of your efforts, you just can't make learning grammar intrinsically and genuinely interesting to students. Mr. Quinn tried; he really did, but even his best efforts ran into serious yawns. What did work was when Mr. Quinn compartmentalized the "stuff that's boring but necessary," as he told them. "Steel yourself, this won't be as good as watching network TV, but you need to know this—so stay with me."

Provide Light for the Adolescent Journey

Adam, as much as any student I ever taught in high school, you were searching to understand how to live a life of integrity, passion, and excellence. You searched into the why of things, the motives and spirit of our nature. Like most young adults I've taught, you were immersed in the weighty, scary, exhilarating project of figuring out who you were, what's possible, to whom you belonged, and what you stood for. For me, the richest and most enduring triumphs in the classroom came when I managed to offer a poem, an essay, a writing assignment, or the space for a discussion that helped light a flare on the path of becoming. These were the moments when students were roused awake.

Mr. Quinn created these moments by fashioning powerful connections between the subject matter and his students. It's important to acknowledge that the default response of the students was to resist these experiences. When Mr. Quinn introduced *Huck Finn* to the class, they approached it as something to be tamed and figured out with minimum effort. As one student told me, "I'll level with you. I liked the first chapter, but I've seen the movie and bought the Cliff Notes so I'm not reading it anymore." Many of the students in Mr. Quinn's class had well-honed strategies for what Denise Pope calls "doing school."[8] Instead of thinking deeply and responding to assignments with intellectual zest, they devote their effort to just squeaking by.

In spite of a prevailing ethos to just "do school" and elude the hard work, students occasionally did so. Mr. Quinn worked relentlessly to create pathways for them to find relevance, utility, and beauty in the subject studied.

Teach with questions, not with answers.
I came to appreciate that when Mr. Quinn was teaching at his best, he was thinking in questions. He would often begin class by drop-

ping a big, luminous question and then letting it work the room. The students appreciated Mr. Quinn's incessant questions as well. "Mr. Quinn, he's like the Sphinx," said one student. When I asked him to explain, he said, "Well, you know, Mr. Quinn is really smart, but he uses his wisdom to make us think, rather than telling us the answers." Mr. Quinn continually asked himself, "What questions can I ask students and what activities can I plan that will allow them to get inside the text?" In watching him work, I believe he used four strategies to make this happen.

First, he devised questions and activities so that the text became a portal through which a social or cultural issue could be discussed. An example of this approach was the class discussion on the use of the word "nigger." Mr. Quinn invited students to think about the state of race relations in their community through the context of *Huck Finn*. Aside from specifically designed assignments, Mr. Quinn was fond of asking questions that linked literature to contemporary issues. For example, when the class was reading *Cannery Row*, he asked, "What would John Steinbeck say about diversity issues in modern America?" When they were studying the poetry of Langston Hughes, he asked, "How would Hughes critique the education that students of color receive at Stanton?"

Second, he used literature and writing activities to encourage students to reflect about their own personal circumstances. A compelling example of this involves the class's encounter with the poem "Barbie Doll." Another day he asked, "With whom would Huck Finn hang out at Stanton? Would he hang out with you? Why? What does that say about you?"

Aside from discussion, Mr. Quinn used journal writing, small-group conversations, and activities like the *Huck Finn* mandala. As one student said, "I like the story about Huck, but what I found more interesting was how the mandala assignment made me think about my own journey. I'm not heading down the Mississippi, but connecting each stage of life that Huck experienced with my own helped me think about my own journey as well."

A third and important way that he fostered a connection between the content and students was that he treated them as if they were connoisseurs of art who were capable of sophisticated responses and evaluations of their encounters with it. He treated the content not as subject matter to be merely mastered but as aesthetic objects to be experienced by discriminating teenagers.

Mr. Quinn also celebrated the immediate delight possible with subject matter. Sometimes he began class with a comment like this: "Driving in this morning, I had the tape player on, and I was listening to this writer Kathleen Norris, and I just got swept up in the grace of her words. I was so moved that I almost had to pull over." He explicitly found ways to remind students that finding genuine enjoyment in their encounters with the subject matter was an indispensable feature of his curriculum. He often asked students, "Did you enjoy reading that? What did you enjoy about that? How did that make you feel?" These questions elevated the subject matter and made it more than just work.

Capitalize on their passion for hanging out with one another.
Mr. Quinn used their desire for social interaction to his advantage. He often moved students into small groups to have quick conversations about provocative issues. Often these small-group conversations were generative and were expanded on and developed in the larger group. They read one another's writing. They had not just discussions, but dialogues about provocative questions.

Share your love affair with reading, writing, and learning.
Model your own love and passion for what you teach. Let them know that you're still on a journey, too, and that art and literature provides you with a compass as well. Mr. Quinn often interrupted

class to tell them about some new book or poem he was reading. He would bring his books to class and wave them about. He would lend them to students. He shared his own writing with them and asked them if they had any input. Poetry, books, art, and language were integral to Mr. Quinn. He was an English teacher who lived it, and they valued that in him. He believed that through literate habits he and his students would live better and more fulfilled lives.

Spark Their Desire to Create

Adam, you were like the students I watched. You wrote poetry, got jazzed up when you thought of a new idea, and solicited being part of a discussion about new ideas and fresh perspectives. The students I watched were most alive, most awake, and most vibrant when they were creating or thinking about something new and novel. I can't emphasize how much they desire activities that allow them to express their autonomy and originality. Perhaps Mr. Quinn's greatest gift as a teacher was his ability to set up the workbench with the right tools, the right materials, and just enough support for students to become swept up in the delight of creation.

Brainstorm, brainstorm, and brainstorm.
Fill your curriculum with activities that enhance instant creativity. Mr. Quinn continually asked students to brainstorm, journal, create mind maps, "free write," and visualize. He communicated to students that such activities work to enhance their creative capacity. He put his own creativity to use, too.

Encourage them to bang ideas together.
Devise opportunities for combining thoughts, media, and ideas. He delighted in putting disparate ideas or concepts before students and asking them to make sense of both. For example, he brought in

Lawrence Kohlberg's theory of moral development and had students apply it to *Huck Finn*. He got them to think outside the box.

Provide incubation time.

Whether it was the class in the outfield, asking a question and having students "free write," or having students sketch out the "action" in a poem like Robert Frost's "The Road Less Traveled," Mr. Quinn provided the space, time, opportunity, and direction so students could enjoy a contemplative moment. They appreciated the change of pace, and they often emerged from these experiences with their most incisive ideas and insights.

Cultivate the students' empathic sensibility.

Insist that students look at problems from multiple perspectives. Mr. Quinn encouraged students to expand their views and step into the thinking of another. He asked them to take on the mind-set of different characters in a text.

Make them feel like they own the curriculum.

Design projects with significant choices and autonomy. Mr. Quinn often offered six or seven choices for every project. He would identify the key principle or idea at the core of the assignment but then students could choose how they wanted to present the material.

Don't Forget to Take Care of Yourself

Adam, you are the show, the star, the colossal influence on all that unfolds in your classroom. Of course, I don't mean that you should act like a spoiled diva. Do recognize that within the boundaries of your classroom you are the ultimate decision maker, tone setter, and world shaper. What happens in that space hinges on your presence, passion, intelligence, creativity, energy, and integrity. When you create the conditions that will promote high-octane moments in the classroom, depend on your vitality, your relationships to students, and the imaginative ways you devise to bring young people into an encounter with the subject content you bring to them.

My good friend Parker J. Palmer writes, "Good teachers possess a capacity for connectedness. They are able to weave a complex web of connections among themselves, their subjects, and their students so that students can learn to weave a world for themselves. The methods used by these weavers vary widely: lectures, Socratic dialogues, laboratory experiments, and collaborative problem solving, creative chaos. The connections made by good teachers are held not in their methods but in their hearts—meaning *heart* in its ancient sense, as the place where intellect and emotion and spirit will converge in the human self."[9] Your best teaching will come when there are moments of deep connections with your students and the subject matter. These are the "spots of time" that glow.

Unfortunately, the system in which we work does little to help us flourish as teachers. The bureaucracy, the schedule, and the demands of the institution align in some pernicious conspiracy to exhaust, deplete, and drain. My experience with Mr. Quinn confirmed what I found when I was teaching. Mr. Quinn, like you, teaches almost 135 students. The daily paper load he faces from collecting and reading student work is overwhelming. One week he collected work each day, and we estimated it involved close to 1,110 pages of student work. He believes deeply in the capacity of schools to contribute to both the lives of students and the civic health of our communities. He views his classroom as a pulsing intersection where the books he teaches, the assignments he develops, the conversations he nurtures, and the relationships he cultivates provide students with the sustenance and influence to navigate the bumpy road of late adolescence. You'd like him and you'd respect him. He believes, as you do, that teaching is mighty and worthy work. Yet he struggles to maintain his passion and his ardent commitment to his teaching, which, when all is said and done, is the fuel that heats that glow.

Robert Fried offers one of the best definitions of passionate teaching I know. He writes, "To be a passionate teacher is to be someone in love with a field of knowledge, deeply stirred by issues and ideas that challenge our world, drawn to dilemmas and potentials of the young people who come into class each day—or captivated by all these. A passionate teacher is a teacher who breaks out of the isolation of a classroom, who refuses to submit to apathy or cynicism. I argue that only when teachers bring their passions about learning and about life into their daily work can they dispel the fog of passive compliance or active disinterest that surrounds so many students."[10]

Fried's point is that you must remain alive, engaged, and vital if you are to fashion experiences that rouse students to life. Our first imperative as teachers is to keep heart, retain our verve, and resist the creep of cynicism. As I write in *Stories of the Courage to Teach,* "For us to be inspiring and spirited teachers, we must stay connected with our colleagues, with our students, with the subjects we teach, and ultimately with our own hopes and ideals. When we feel isolated from colleagues, detached from our students and removed from the subjects that we teach, we become disconnected and it is nearly impossible to teach well."[11]

How did Mr. Quinn stay fired up? How did he sustain his presence, passion, and fire despite working within an institution that seemed to leech his best hopes and aspirations? After having watched Mr. Quinn work, I offer several suggestions:

Stay connected with your colleagues.
Resist the urge to close your classroom door and merely do your own thing. Mr. Quinn maintained friendships and collegial connec-

tions with a range of colleagues and he moderated an e-mail list for English teachers around the state. He also found tremendous satisfaction writing about his work for himself and for professional magazines.

Tend your love of content.

Adam, never forget that you're an English teacher and you must continually read and engage with literature. Mr. Quinn incessantly listened to books on tape and read poetry. He lived with his subject matter in ways that felt authentic to students. As one student said, "Mr. Quinn loves poetry and writing and it's sort of contagious."

Streamline—and jaywalk.

Develop rubrics and systems to keep your head above the paper. When Mr. Quinn got behind on the paper, you could literally see his stress and frustration rise. Recognize when you're about to get steamrolled, and move out of the way. Several times during the year, Mr. Quinn felt himself "getting crispy," as he described it, and he took a day to breathe. Call it a mental health day, view it as a day to get college recommendations done, or just stay home and huddle with a book. Nobody benefits if the sheer volume of demands incapacitates you.

Resist the minutia.

Mr. Quinn took great delight in not falling prey to the senseless wheel-spinning that often marked his encounters with the administration. Once returning from a meeting, he whipped out a copy of the *New Yorker* and said, "This saved me. That meeting was so deadly to the heart that if I didn't have this I'd have leapt on the table and started shrieking." He found ways to inoculate himself against these incursions.

Mostly he kept trying and changing and learning and growing.

So, Adam, let me return to your initial question: What did I learn during my sojourn to the back of Mr. Quinn's classroom? In the end, I believe these moments of special luminosity where students stretched upward and grew in mind and spirit are not magical, random events, but episodes cultivated by inspired, artful teaching. A teacher's analogue to a poet's ode or a painter's portrait is the moment when students are tuned in, fired up and brimming over. I also learned that while educational reformers are rightfully concerned with school context and other broad and enduring issues, the classroom is the heart of the educational enterprise. Our beleaguered educational system provides a slue of constraints and impediments that impair a teacher's ability to achieve his or her goals and vision; however, within your classroom you can inspire hope, wonder, and a zest for living and learning.

*   *   *

Fondly,
Sam I.

Author's Note and Methods

In the first chapter I traced the roots of this project back to experiences I had during my first years as a teacher in Brooklyn, New York. I described how my classroom would occasionally become swept up with what I called a spirit of ferocious learning, where students would be engrossed and wide awake. These moments always felt elusive, as if some benevolent sprite had dusted my classroom with magic chalk dust. I would walk out of class wishing that I could capture this lightning in a bottle so I could study what went right and deconstruct the sequence of events. But these moments were more ineffable than understandable, and they always seemed to belie planning and predictability.

Years later the questions still gnaw at me. Thus, I feel privileged to have been able to tackle this study; it's a gift to have the time and resources to chase an intellectual and emotional puzzle. In the end, as I knew before I started, I would find no formula for classroom alchemy and no Betty Crocker recipes for magical chalk dust. But over the course of this study, I came to believe that if we aspire to create classrooms where our adolescents are engrossed, emotionally stimulated, and with their minds wide awake then we need to recalibrate a fundamental precept at every level of our educational thinking. We've become preoccupied with the destination of education, but for the teachers and students who trudge off to classrooms every day it's the journey that counts. Teachers viscerally understand

Dewey's claim that, "It is better to travel than to arrive, it is because traveling is a constant arriving."[1]

In the end, this study revealed experiences where students stretched upward and grew in mind and spirit. They felt alive in the classroom. They were excited, passionate, and inspired by their academic tasks. These compelling events may routinely elude our reach, but teaching is a continuous experiment and an ongoing series of compositions, each a draft, where much is possible. Despite the constraints we often face within our institutions, we must imagine our classrooms as powerful and humane spaces. Implicit in this point is a call to hope, to wonder, and to cling to the belief that teachers can forge a classroom where meaningful, enduring work will be done.

I began this project thinking that I would study the classrooms of multiple teachers so that I could compare episodes of inspired learning and potent teaching from one context to the next. During a preliminary study, I observed six different teachers and six classrooms. Over the course of this pilot study, I realized that it was difficult to trace the ebb and flow of student experience and teacher decision-making if I wasn't fully immersed in the classroom every day. This realization convinced me to focus my efforts on a single classroom.

This decision was made based on two criteria. First, it was imperative to develop an intimate knowledge of the ordinary rhythms and procedures of the classroom while cultivating a deep rapport with the class and the teacher. Many of the experiences students shared with me involved deeply personal dimensions of their lives. I needed to gain the students' trust, and that entailed being present in class every day and finding ways to connect with them outside of class as well. Second, an assumption of this study is that many of the most enduring effects of classroom life unfold during the days, weeks, and months that students and teachers are together. Understanding the shared history of a classroom was an imperative feature of this work. I needed to be there every day.

An important question that I am often asked about the work is how did I discriminate between an elevated episode and one that is good but routine? My analytic method involved three steps. First, I relied on my own perception of what was happening in the classroom. If I felt a general sense of attention, focus, and emotional intensity in the classroom, I would signal to Mr. Quinn to distribute index cards so we could conduct a reflective prompt. Students would write 50–100 words answering this question: Describe what you were thinking and feeling during class today. A typical response would read as follows: "I came into class thinking about this math test that I probably bombed second period. I was pretty distracted, but then Mr. Quinn put on that classical music and asked us to write about the passage in Nathan McCall's book. I started writing about how there are so many traps for teenagers to fall into today—fights, drugs, unsafe sex, gambling. Then we started talking about that. I was really into it and forgot a lot of other stuff in my head."

Early in the study I determined that if more than half the students described being focused and emotionally involved in what was happening in class, then I would consider it to be an episode of inspired learning. Using this metric, I determined that of the 128 classes I observed, there were 22 episodes of inspired learning, which is about 18 percent.

Importantly, there were times that individual students experienced episodes of inspired learning; however, these episodes did not qualify for inclusion in the study. For example, during one class session one group of students had a riveting conversation about their future during a discussion of Robert Frost's poem "The Road Not Taken." I observed that group, but when I distributed the reflective prompts the majority of the class did not describe being focused and absorbed. This episode was clearly profound for the one group, but I do not include it in the 22.

Once I identified an episode as an example of inspired learning, I conducted follow-up interviews with Mr. Quinn and students. I used three predominant modes of data collection: structured interviewing, where I adhered to a pre-designed interview schedule; open questioning, where I followed the lead and flow of the conversation;

and structured questioning, where I pursued an individual's reflections on an episode by asking, "Tell me more about your thoughts" or "Can you describe what you experienced?"[2] Mr. Quinn and I also devised several writing assignments that invited students to think systematically about their reactions to and feelings around these episodes.

As I collected the data, I analyzed it following what qualitative researchers call an ongoing, cyclical, inductive process of discerning patterns and themes. I joked with friends that my research demanded me to become a combination of Pat Summerall and John Madden, the football broadcasters, in that my role was to give the play-by-play of what happened in the classroom, and simultaneously give the color commentary and explain why events transpired the way they did, how they came about, and why they were significant. The portraits of the episodes, which constitute the heart of this book, can be read in this spirit.

An important question to address is whether this study has generalizability, which is a researcher's term for whether what I found can be broadly applied. It's a valid and important question, but it is one that I think is difficult to address in the language of methodology, which is often opaque and dense around these issues. I am reminded of a simile offered by Chris Clark, a former teacher turned researcher, who wrote, "Teaching is like a story, like a journey. Story and journey are familiar patterns with infinite variations. Each story and each journey is special, distinct from all others. Yet all stories share some common features, as do journeys."[3]

I began my teaching career in an inner-city high school in Brooklyn and then moved to Vermont where I taught at a rural high school set in a cow pasture. I also served as the dean of students at a top-tier suburban high school and now teach in a liberal arts college. I know firsthand that enormous differences exist among schools and students in America, but I also fervidly believe that Chris Clarke has it right: teaching is a story, and all stories share common features. I believe the story told here will share common features with your school, your students, and you. I hope you enjoyed the journey.

Notes

Chapter 1: "The Kids Were on Fire"

1. Margaret Metzger, "Maintaining a Life: Calling in the Cosmos," *Phi Delta Kappan* (1996): 346–51.

2. Larry Cuban, "Reflections on a Career in Teaching," in *Reflections: Personal Essays by Thirty-three Distinguished Educators*, ed. Derek L. Burleson (Bloomington, Ind.: Phi Delta Kappa Educational Foundation, 1991), 68.

3. Annie Dillard, *The Annie Dillard Reader* (New York: Harper Collins, 1994).

4. Mike Rose, *Possible Lives: The Promise of Public Education in America* (Boston: Houghton Mifflin, 1995), 4.

5. N. Scott Momaday, *The Way to Rainy Mountain* (Albuquerque: University of New Mexico Press, 1969), 83.

Chapter 2: Spans of Time That Don't Glow

1. See John Goodlad, *A Place Called School: Prospects for the Future* (New York: McGraw-Hill, 1984), 9. For other examples of research studies documenting the modal state of American high school classrooms see Mihaly Csikszentmihalyi and Reed Larson, *Being Adolescent: Conflict and Growth in the Teenage Years* (New York: Basic, 1984), 66, where they conclude that "compared to other contexts in their lives, time in class is associated with lower-than-average states on nearly every self-report dimension. Most notably, students report feeling sad, irritable, and bored; concentration is difficult; they feel self-conscious and strongly wish they were doing something else. . . . Even in a very good high school, such as the one studied here, students are neither attentive nor happy,

and are probably absorbing only a fraction of the information being presented."
Also, Theodore Sizer, *Horace's Compromise: The Dilemma of the American High
School* (New York: Houghton Mifflin, 1984); and A. Powell, D. Cohen, and T.
Farrar, *The Shopping Mall High School: Winners and Losers in the Educational
Marketplace* (New York: Houghton Mifflin, 1985).

Chapter 3: Seeing the World in a Plot of Grass

1. John Steinbeck, *Cannery Row* (New York: Penguin, 1945), 1.

2. Elliot Eisner, *Cognition and Curriculum Reconsidered*, 2d ed. (New
York: Teachers College Press, 1994), 18.

3. John Dewey, *Art as Experience* (New York: Perigree, 1934), 52. Also see
Elliot W. Eisner, *The Arts and the Creation of Mind* (New Haven: Yale University
Press, 2002), 35–38.

4. Dewey, *Art as Experience*, 53.

5. M. Regina Leffers, "Pragmatists Jane Addams and John Dewey Inform
the Ethic of Care," *Hypatia* 8, no. 2 (1993): 64–77, 72.

6. Charles Taylor, *Sources of the Self: The Making of the Modern Identity*
(Cambridge: Harvard University Press, 1989), 419.

7. Morris Beja, *Epiphany in the Modern Novel* (Seattle: University of
Washington Press, 1971), 19.

8. Dewey, *Art as Experience*, 21.

9. James C. Collins and Jerry I. Porras, *Built to Last: Successful Habits of
Visionary Companies* (New York: Harper Business, 1994), 54.

10. Collins and Porras, *Built to Last*, 54.

11. David Hargreaves, *Deviance in the Classroom* (London: Routledge,
1975), 2.

12. Anthony Storr, *Solitude: A Return to the Self* (New York: Free Press,
1988), 21.

Chapter 4: Forging Community

1. John Steinbeck, *The Grapes of Wrath* (New York: Viking, 1939).

2. Victor Turner, "The Center out There: Pilgrim's Goal," *History of Religions* 12, no. 3 (1973): 216.

3. Victor Turner, *The Ritual Process: Structure and Anti-Structure* (Chicago:
Aldine, 1969), 28.

4. Turner, *Ritual Process*, 128.

5. See Arthur N. Applebee, *Curriculum as Conversation: Transforming Traditions of Teaching and Learning* (Chicago: University of Chicago Press, 1996).

6. Parker J. Palmer, *The Courage to Teach: Exploring the Inner Landscape of a Teacher's Life* (San Francisco: Jossey-Bass, 1998), 76.

7. For elaboration on the processes of classroom talk, see Courtney B. Cazden, *Classroom Discourse: The Language of Teaching and Learning* (Portsmouth, N.H.: Heinemann, 1988), 29–41. Cazden presents a detailed example of a classroom transcript that brings to high relief the automaticity of this pattern. See also Hugh Mehan, *Learning Lessons: Social Organization in the Classroom* (Cambridge: Harvard University Press, 1979); and Nicholas C. Burbules, *Dialogue in Teaching: Theory and Practice*, vol. 10 (New York: Teachers College Press, 1993).

8. See, for example, A. A. Bellack, *The Language of the Classroom* (New York: Teachers College Press), 1966.

Chapter 5: Grasping Insight

1. John W. Gardner, *Self-Renewal: The Individual and the Innovative Society* (New York: Norton, 1981), 13.

2. Gardner, *Self-Renewal*, 13.

3. Michael Polyani, *The Study of Man* (Chicago: University of Chicago Press, 1959), 28.

4. Edward Hirsch, *How to Read a Poem: And Fall in Love with Poetry* (New York: Harcourt Brace, 1999), 5.

5. Wolfgang Iser, *The Act of Reading: A Theory of Aesthetic Response* (Baltimore: Johns Hopkins University Press, 1978), 79.

6. Nathan McCall, *Makes Me Wanna Holler: A Young Black Man in America* (New York: Random House, 1994).

7. Paulo Freire, *Pedagogy of the Oppressed* (New York: Continuum), 1970.

8. Freire, *Pedagogy*, 69.

9. See, for example, Arthur N. Applebee, *Curriculum as Conversation: Transforming Traditions of Teaching and Learning* (Chicago: University of Chicago Press, 1996); and Richard Beach and Susan Hynds, "Research on Response to Literature," in *Handbook of Reading Research*, edited by Rebecca Barr, David Pearson, Michael L. Kamil, and Peter Mosenthal (New York: Longman, 1991), 453–89; and Alan Purves, *Reading and Literature: American Achievement in International Perspective* (Urbana, Ill.: National Council of Teachers of English, 1981).

10. Martha Nussbaum, *Love's Knowledge* (Oxford: Oxford University Press, 1990), 5.

11. See Purves, *Reading and Literature*. This study found a high correlation between literature in a vernacular, familiar tone and reports of student enjoyment.

12. See, for example, Maxine Greene, *Releasing the Imagination: Essays on Education, the Arts, and Social Change* (San Francisco: Jossey-Bass, 1995); Rachael Kessler, *The Soul of Education: Helping Students Find Connection, Compassion, and Character at School* (Alexandria, Va.: Association for Supervision and Curriculum Development, 2000); and David E. Purpel, *The Moral and Spiritual Crisis in Education* (New York: Bergin and Garvey, 1989).

13. Katherine G. Simon, *Moral Questions in the Classroom: How to Get Kids to Think Deeply About Real Life and Their Schoolwork* (New Haven: Yale University Press, 2001), 54–99.

14. Kenneth Koch, "The Language of Poetry," *New York Review of Books,* May 14, 1998, 83–84.

Chapter 6: Doing Good

1. See Bertrand Russell, *The Conquest of Happiness* (New York: Bantam, 1968).

2. For further exploration of the dimensions of eudaemonia, see the following: John Kekes, *Moral Wisdom and Good Lives* (Ithaca: Cornell University Press, 1995), especially his chapter "The Shadow of a Eudaemonist"; Gregory Vlastos, "Happiness and Virtue in Socrates' Moral Theory," *Proceedings of the Cambridge Philological Society* 30 (1984): 181–213; also, Martha Nussbaum, *The Fragility of Goodness: Luck and Ethics in Greek Tragedy and Philosophy* (Cambridge: Cambridge University Press, 1986). Nussbaum contends in the chapter "The Vulnerability of the Good Human Life: Activity and Disaster" that the eudaemonic experience necessitates action, or actual activity, rather than just a state of good character. Last, see Robin Barrow, *Happiness* (Oxford: Martin Robertson, 1980), 15–26.

3. Aristotle, *Nicomachean Ethics,* trans. Martin Ostwald (Indianapolis: Bobbs-Merrill, 1962), 286.

4. Robert Coles, *The Call of Service: A Witness to Idealism* (Boston: Houghton Mifflin, 1993), 74.

5. Robert Nozick, *Philosophical Explanations* (Cambridge: Harvard University Press, 1981), 586.

6. J. D. Salinger, *The Catcher in the Rye* (New York: Bantam, 1945), 173.

7. See, for example, Nel Noddings, *Caring: A Feminine Approach to Ethics and Moral Education* (Berkeley: University of California Press, 1984); and Nel Noddings, *The Challenge to Care in Schools* (New York: Teachers College Press, 1992); and Milton Mayeroff, *On Caring* (New York: Harper and Row, 1971).

8. See, for example, Mihaly Csikszentmihalyi and Reed Larson, *Being Adolescent: Conflict and Growth in the Teenage Years* (New York: Basic, 1984);

and Susan Harter, "Self and Identity Development," in *At the Threshold: The Developing Adolescent,* ed. S. Shirley Feldman and Glen R. Elliott (Cambridge: Harvard University Press, 1990), 352–87.

9. See, for example, Albert Bandura, *Self-Efficacy: The Exercise of Control* (New York: W. H. Freeman, 1996).

10. Bandura, *Self-Efficacy.*

11. Bandura, *Self-Efficacy,* 36.

12. See, for example, Jennie Oakes, *Keeping Track: How Schools Structure Inequality* (New Haven: Yale University Press, 1985).

13. See, for example, Philip Wexler, *Becoming Somebody: Toward a Social Psychology of School* (London: Falmer, 1992).

14. See Jim Garrison, *Dewey and Eros: Wisdom and Desire in the Art of Teaching* (New York: Teachers College Press, 1997).

15. See, for example, Harry H. Vorrath and Larry K. Brendtro, *Positive Peer Culture* (New York: Aldine, 1985).

Chapter 7: Tangling with the Unspeakable

1. See Mary Budd Rowe, "Wait Time: Slowing Down May Be a Way of Speeding Up," *American Educator* 47 (1987): 38–43.

2. Michelle Fine, *Framing Dropouts: Notes on the Politics of an Urban Public High School* (Albany: State University of New York Press, 1991), 32.

3. Maxine Greene, *Releasing the Imagination: Essays on Education, the Arts, and Social Change* (San Francisco: Jossey-Bass, 1995).

4. Theodore Sizer, "On the Habit of Informed Skepticism," in *Teaching for Intelligence: A Collection of Articles,* ed. Barbara Z. Presseisen (Arlington Heights, Ill.: Skylight Professional Development, 1999), 16.

5. Jim Garrison, *Dewey and Eros: Wisdom and Desire in the Art of Teaching,* ed. Jonas F. Soltis (New York: Teachers College Press, 1997), 115.

6. Parker J. Palmer, *The Courage to Teach: Exploring the Inner Landscape of a Teacher's Life* (San Francisco: Jossey-Bass, 1998), 110.

7. Tom Peters and Nancy Austin, *A Passion for Excellence: The Leadership Difference* (New York: Random House, 1985), 284.

8. Howard Gardner, *Leading Minds: An Anatomy of Leadership* (New York: Basic, 1995), 55.

9. See Leila Christenbury and Pat Kelly, *Making the Journey* (Portsmouth, N.H.: Heinemann, 2000).

10. bell hooks, *Teaching to Transgress: Education as the Practice of Freedom* (New York: Routledge, 1994), 13.

11. Greene, *Releasing the Imagination,* 19.

Chapter 8: Caught!

1. Joseph Campbell, with Bill Moyers, Betty Sue Flowers, ed. *The Power of Myth* (New York: Doubleday, 1988).

2. Philip Levine, *What Work Is* (New York: Knopf, 1997).

3. William James, *The Principles of Psychology*, vol. 1 (New York: Henry Holt, 1890), 403–404.

4. See the introduction to a recent special issue (spring 2002, vol. 37, no. 2) of the journal *Educational Psychologist* that devotes a full edition to emotions in education. The editors write: "As motivation, cognitive, developmental, and educational psychologists have continued to contextualize their inquiry within the schools, it has become clear that emotions are an integral part of educational activity settings. In the 2000s, researchers interested in teaching, learning, and motivational transactions within the classroom context can no longer ignore emotional issues. Emotions are intimately involved in virtually every aspect of the teaching and learning process and, therefore, an understanding of the nature of emotions within the school context is essential."

5. See Israel Scheffler, *In Praise of the Cognitive Emotions and Other Essays in the Philosophy of Education* (New York: Routledge, 1991).

6. See Martha Nussbaum, *Upheavals of Thought: The Intelligence of Emotions* (Cambridge: Cambridge University Press, 2001), 4.

7. Nussbaum, *Upheavals of Thought*, 30–31.

8. Parker J. Palmer, *The Courage to Teach: Exploring the Inner Landscape of a Teacher's Life* (San Francisco: Jossey-Bass, 1998).

9. Nussbaum, *Upheavals of Thought*, 31.

10. Alfred Whitehead, *Aims of Education* (New York: Macmillan, 1929), 1.

11. Robert Nozick, *The Examined Life: Philosophical Meditations* (New York: Touchstone, 1989), 39.

12. Thomas H. Naylor, William H. Willimon, and Magdalena R. Naylor, *The Search for Meaning* (Nashville: Abingdon, 1994), 96.

Chapter 9: A Letter to a Colleague

1. William Ayers, *To Become a Teacher: Making a Difference in Children's Lives* (New York: Teachers College Press, 1995), x.

2. Theodore R. Sizer, *Horace's School: Redesigning the American High School* (Boston: Houghton Mifflin, 1992), 41.

3. Elissa Moses, *The $100 Billion Allowance: Accessing the Global Teen Market* (New York: John Wiley, 2000).

4. A. Bartlett Giamatti, *Take Time for Paradise: Americans and Their Games* (New York: Summit, 1989).

5. Moses, *$100 Billion Allowance*, 44–45

6. Thomas H. Davenport and John C. Beck, *The Attention Economy: Understanding the New Currency of Business* (Boston: Harvard Business School, 2001), 218.

7. Seymour Sarason, *Teaching as Performing Art* (New York: Teachers College Press, 1999), 15.

8. Denise Clark Pope, *"Doing School": How We Are Creating a Generation of Stressed Out, Materialistic, and Miseducated Students* (New Haven: Yale University Press, 2001).

9. Parker J. Palmer, *The Courage to Teach: Exploring the Inner Landscape of a Teacher's Life* (San Francisco: Jossey-Bass, 1998), 11.

10. Robert L. Fried, *The Passionate Teacher: A Practical Guide* (Boston: Beacon, 1995), 1.

11. Sam M. Intrator, *Stories of the Courage to Teach: Honoring the Teacher's Heart* (San Francisco: Jossey-Bass, 2002), 282.

Author's Note and Methods

1. John Dewey, *Human Nature and Conduct: An Introduction to Social Psychology* (New York: Henry Holt, 1922), 282.

2. Corrine Glesne and Alan Peshkin, *Becoming Qualitative Researchers* (White Plains: Longman, 1992).

3. Christopher Clark, *Thoughtful Teaching* (New York: Teachers College Press, 1995), xv.

Index